T0128282

POWER
— TO GET —
WEALTH

RANDY PARLOR

WESTBOW
PRESS®
A DIVISION OF THOMAS NELSON
& ZONDERVAN

Copyright © 2020 Randy Parlor.

All rights reserved. No part of this book may be used or reproduced by
any means, graphic, electronic, or mechanical, including photocopying,
recording, taping or by any information storage retrieval system
without the written permission of the author except in the case of
brief quotations embodied in critical articles and reviews.

WestBow Press books may be ordered through booksellers or by contacting:

WestBow Press
A Division of Thomas Nelson & Zondervan
1663 Liberty Drive
Bloomington, IN 47403
www.westbowpress.com
844-714-3454

Because of the dynamic nature of the Internet, any web addresses or
links contained in this book may have changed since publication and
may no longer be valid. The views expressed in this work are solely those
of the author and do not necessarily reflect the views of the publisher,
and the publisher hereby disclaims any responsibility for them.

Any people depicted in stock imagery provided by Getty Images are
models, and such images are being used for illustrative purposes only.
Certain stock imagery © Getty Images.

Scripture quotations marked NKJV are taken from the New King James Version®.
Copyright © 1982 by Thomas Nelson. Used by permission. All rights reserved.

ISBN: 978-1-6642-0642-7 (sc)
ISBN: 978-1-6642-0643-4 (hc)
ISBN: 978-1-6642-0641-0 (e)

Library of Congress Control Number: 2020918312

Print information available on the last page.

WestBow Press rev. date: 10/29/2020

CONTENTS

*A sound plan & process based on principles noted
above to eliminate financial bondage and build wealth*

PRELUDE

I am the Author of four biblical financial books, editor of two books written by Karen Parlor, my wife, and author of hundreds of MoneyWalk articles. Our eBooks are available on Amazon and Google Books. Articles and videos can be found at Facebook, Linkedin, Google Blogger, Pinterest, Tumblr, Twitter, WordPress, and YouTube. When we started on the path to bettering our finances in 1992, we had debt of $135,000 and a negative $35,000 net worth. We tithed and gave abundantly while working our way out of financial bondage. By the LORD's grace we have been constructively debt-free since 1998 and are now multi-millionaires via budgeting, giving, saving, debt-free living, and no-load low-expense stock index mutual fund investing. We were career public servants working for state government and a state university. In 2018 (our mid-fifties) *we retired, yet continue to engage entrepreneurial and ministry endeavors like teaching people how to manage money entrusted to them. We believe sharing the good news with people, giving to spread the gospel, and following biblical financial principles open huge doors of prosperity that help us and others fulfill God-given purpose.*

The first thing you need to know is the LORD Jesus Christ wants you healthy, wealthy, and wise including financial prosperity that helps you, in a greater way, evangelize, make disciples, and serve others. Deuteronomy 8:18 contains a promise that is available for Christians just like it was for Old Testament believers. It is clear that the ability is not in and of yourself, rather it is the LORD who gives you power to get wealth, so you can establish His covenant in the earth. This means sharing the gospel with everyone and taking dominion over the earth in ways He designed. In Christ you can take authority over finances. According to the way He designed the parameters of our world and possibilities in it, the greatest dominion will only be possible when you use the power He gave you to get wealth He has for you in Heaven and bring it down for fruitfulness on earth that glorifies Him and is a blessing to others in ways that lead them to Him and make their lives better.

His promises throughout the bible have to do with you being the joy set before Him for which He died to save and give eternal life before the foundation of the world was laid. Also, they have to do with the unmerited favor He gave you by which you can be free via grace through faith in Him by choosing to accept His gift of salvation and eternal life. This cannot be earned by good works or any ability you could muster. In addition, they have to do with the fact that true faith in Him will move you to follow the guidance of the Holy Spirit to do everything Father God purposed for you in Christ to help evangelize and make disciples of as many other people as possible while you remain upon this earth. Therefore, He desires that you follow His instruction to increase money and resources in your life in ways that glorify Him while walking out this adventure of leading your family, friends, neighbors, coworkers, and many others to Him via your example of intimacy with Him and using the various giftings, abilities, and skills He imparts to you in service to them.

We accepted Jesus Christ as Savior & LORD on June 29, 1992 and realized we needed to look to Him and the bible for inspiration to find our purpose and to find out if He had anything to say about our financial predicament that could help us know if we needed to change the way we were managing money He entrusts to us. Via praying and listening to Him we followed the instruction to tithe and give an offering as a catalyst to working our way out of financial bondage.

We have been able to condense our twenty-seven years of learning and experience into ELEVEN BIBLICAL PRINCIPLES and SEVEN STEPS TO FINANCIAL FREEDOM & WEALTH, which immensely help everyone who chooses to use them because they are based upon biblical guidance. Moving forward would not be eternally worthwhile or of earthly good to us without employing other disciplines the LORD instructs us to follow for our betterment. These disciplines are *(1)* Worshipping throughout each day via thanksgiving, praise, and prayer, *(2)* Studying the bible, both new and old testaments to know and understand the whole counsel of the LORD and thereby to walk in wisdom in everything we say and do, *(3)* Fellowshipping and serving with other believers *(via a local Church)* who engage the first two disciplines on a regular basis and who desire to be Christ-like for the remainder of their lives on earth, *(4)* Declaring what the LORD said in the bible as truth no matter what the surrounding culture says is politically correct, *(5)* Letting faith move us to action by engaging our part in the Great Commandment & Commission given to us and every believer whose lives are hidden in Jesus Christ. These disciplines in combination with the eleven principles and focused seven-step plan will take you to The Wealthy Place.

Anything less *(even if you accumulate all the money in the world)* is meaningless because it profits no one to gain the world, yet lose his / her soul in the process. The LORD's will should always be the number one priority of your life, from which all other priorities flow. To Him, your worth is not based on the amount of assets you accumulate on earth. He loves you just as you are but wants to provide more for you to be a blessing to other people and to help fund the gospel throughout the earth. Earthly income and assets have no bearing on your worth or His love, yet *(when His will is your priority)* higher income allows you to give, save, and spend more in ways that glorify Him.

I have been extremely poor, raised by a single mother with three older brothers, all one year apart, living in a city far away from extended family, with almost no contact with or help from them for many years. My mother was God-fearing and raised us in the light of the gospel and we got to see her walk with the LORD get better as time progressed. She was diagnosed as disabled most of her adult life and thus we lived on welfare until I was grown. By the grace of God, later in life she was able to receive Social Security from her estranged husband who did not divorce her. I had three brothers and each of us had different fathers. I am the youngest. My oldest brother was four years older than me. He died at 43 and my second oldest brother died at 31.

Our fathers, their extended families, and our half brothers and sisters never tried to make contact with us or reciprocate contact we made. Mom taught us many good things and exampled for us how to do work that you could do *(via her intimacy with the LORD and rearing us to honor and respect Him and His discipline)*. Our immediate family was all alone in Michigan and for the most part only had regular contact from our maternal Grandfather from Alabama who would talk to us on the phone every few months and visit about once every five-years.

Mom ensured that we cleaned, dusted, washed dishes, and had other chores everyday alongside her. We were not allowed to half-do any of the chores so we could live properly as good citizens when we became adults. She kept us in school and made sure we did our homework and chores before we could go out and play. She cooked big meals pretty much every day and fed us and other people in the neighborhood. She was the greatest cook I know – Chef Willie P. I miss her so much since she died, but always cherish the many godly lessons she taught us while facing a hard life, harsh obstacles, painful trials, and a lonely road for many years.

If I had only followed much of her example early in my adult life I would never have been in financial trouble. She made each of us go get work permits when we were fourteen so we could get summer jobs and encouraged us long before this to cut neighbors' grass, shovel their snow, and do other little odd jobs we could help them with. She never asked us for any of our pay as dues for staying in the home, but as we progressed in our teens, she let us know some desires above the basics of food, clothing, and a place to stay would be our responsibility during seasons when we could work.

She also let us know we should always tithe and save some money even though she couldn't save much with the welfare we received. She took us to the bank at a young age to open savings accounts. Mom told us every day she loved us, each one individually. We willingly wanted to give a portion of our earnings to help in any way we could. Life in the Parlor home was grand even though we did not have much compared to many others. Yet, we had the love of the LORD and our Mom and access through Him to everything we needed and more even though we had to pray and sometimes wait for due season to reap and/or receive it.

We never owned a house. We were renters moving every few years to different parts of Ypsilanti and then to Lansing. We never owned a car. My second oldest brother Darryl bought a used Ford LTD for a couple of hundred dollars in 1979 when he was nineteen. It did not last long because he did not really know how to take care of it and the repair costs were beyond his ability to continue to pay at the time. I *(the youngest sibling)* became the first in my immediate family to purchase a new car *(Ford Escort)* in the summer I graduated from college. However, I was aimed by my own desires and other people down the wrong road and would end up feeling the negative effects of debt *(and high finance charges that accompany it)* because I continued to purchase many expensive and unnecessary products and services *(given my annual pay)* via loans creditors were very willing to give me.

I did not understand that compound interest works against you with regard to finance charges on loans in the same way compound interest works for you on investments gains. Both are expressed as annual interest, yet it generally results in growth on investments versus money you are paying a creditor on top of the principle loan amount.

For example, if you invested $10,000 and earned 10% compounded annually for 20 years your asset would grow to $67,275.

However, if you took out a $10,000 loan that charged 10% interest *(finance charge)* and you did not make payments on it for 20 years your debt would grow to $67,275.

Even when you make minimum principle and interest payments on the loan over a period of three, five, or more years, the creditor will charge you thousands of dollars, which is money you cannot use to eliminate debt or invest for wealth building.

The saddest part about this predicament is finance charges on loans are usually far higher than interest or growth you can make on investments. Thus, you are put further behind the eight-ball each and every time you take out debt to finance lifestyle. Most people do not take loans out to cover the purchase of products or services that appreciate in value. Thus, loans for most items are for depreciating assets that lose value over time. These cause your loan balance for many years to be far higher than the value of the item the loan was used to purchase. Again, they take a lot of years to pay off because of the great amount of interest you will pay the creditor.

I was living like everyone around me and thus I was not in a good situation throughout my twenty's. I started by getting student loans in my senior year. I did not need them, because I had a full-ride basketball scholarship. However, I got them anyway simply because I was told they were available. I understand research suggests people spend about 38% more than they otherwise would when they use debt to finance purchases. Also, college students spend about a third of student loans on non-school purchases *(lifestyle, clothing, eating out, etc.)*. I did both of these in the undisciplined portion of my life. My scholarship essentially meant the federal government Pell Grant and other grants paid most of my undergraduate expenses *(room, board, tuition, books, and necessary meals)*. The university made student athletes apply for federal aid and would only pay necessary costs above those paid by grants and scholarships.

My family was monetarily poor and thus I received everything needed via grants and scholarships. In addition, every year I could get several thousand dollars of work study grant money as long as I could find employment around the campus, which I had no problem doing when my schedule allowed and I wanted to. However, my habits increasingly led me to want to party instead of work and also desire more money than was provided by grants, scholarships, and work study so I could hang out with friends and buy stuff I did not need to impress people including some of whom I did not even like.

I got so bad I started calling my desires needs because that would make it more palatable to spend what was not really mine and to feel good about it even though it was increasingly drowning me in debt as the years moved on. I always say the pleasures of sin are insidious. They do not look like a problem when you first take action to obtain them but they increasingly cause more problems because the desire for them starts ruling your decision-making and sin becomes more noticeably negative until you feel overwhelmed, like you cannot stop the train *(negative consequences)* from running over you. Debt bondage is insidious in the same manner. I did not need the student loans and the debt lingered for many years after college and I had nothing positive to show for it. I looked good on the outside but on the inside of my life *(the part people could not see at that time)* my poor financial stewardship was causing my world to crumble and creating stress and pressure.

I married my sweetheart, but continued the poor financial pattern. I still longed for the same things. I just wanted to add her into my mix. She was unable to change me and also was not looking to the LORD for her life or financial stewardship at that time. We were drifting along like pieces of dry wood going wherever the current took us instead of being intentional with meaningful plans for our life. The craving for things, pleasures, and popularity among worldly friends put me in bondage to debt and led me to continue unwise decision-making. We finally realized on June 29, 1992 that we were in over our heads and could not get out of the trouble on our own, but even more important we realized that we need the only

Savior, Jesus Christ the LORD, to save us, grant us eternal life, and help us live in a much better, purpose-filled, fruitful way while we are on Earth.

This took the shackles off our feet, so we could dance. It freed us to start studying the bible to find out the principles that the LORD wants people to apply to their lives. I did not really know He had anything to say in this regard, but I finally realized He cares for me so the bible must contain guidance concerning every area of my life to help me navigate the land mines of this world and the deceit of satan. This would keep my feet on good solid ground that produces blessing and reward.

I found out that He has much to say about our stewardship, the management of resources entrusted to us. At first, it was difficult to accept some of His instruction because some of it is different from what I had been socialized to believe and do by the culture and society around me. Yet, I asked the Holy Spirit to help me persevere in seeking and obeying His instruction. Step by step he helped me over the past 25 years follow Him instead of the world. I have had a few relapses along the way, in terms of unwise financial choices, but He pulled me back in and showed me the error of my ways and set my feet on a rock to stay so I would have Him and His ways as a firm foundation upon which to make better choices as I move forward in life. He made my wife the help-meat every husband needs and should truly want because her attitude, demeanor, and wisdom help guide our lifestyle and financial decisions in a way that makes the LORD and His will the center of our life.

The following chapters are a synopsis of the pathway the bible pointed us to for good stewardship as well as methods and tools that fit within biblical principles. It is not the only way to prosper financially while on Earth, but it is a way that will bring focus to your endeavor to straighten out your life and break financial bondage. Certainly, other people may have plans you could follow that may be just as good as the Eleven Principles and Seven-Step plan I will describe. However, this plan is very simple to follow. Many other plans are much too difficult to follow intellectually and make people feel as if they have to be a math nerd or financial wizard. Thus, most people don't stick with them through the course of their lives or jump around from one plan to another and do not make much of a change in their lives or finances. This unfortunately is the result of trying to follow every wind of doctrine. The vast majority of people, when faced with too many choices, feel as if they cannot choose a few focused ones and put them together in a way that would benefit them. So, they tend to become immobilized by the array of choices all the speakers, conferences, workshops, books, tapes, mp3's, etc. show them and thus do nothing to better their situation.

It is better to find a concise plan *(like the one in this book)* that conforms to biblical principles and utilize it to get out of bondage and build wealth. The Seven-Step plan I will share is based on steps the LORD walked us up in the early 1990's to get out of financial bondage and become multi-millionaires, even though in some people's eyes we were lowly public servants. I guide others up this path and many of them have also broken bondage and built wealth by learning to be good stewards of manifold resources He entrusts to them. He is allowing me to share this ladder of progression with you in a concise manner so you do not have to wonder where you are headed and if it works.

When your expenses are consistently more than your net income you experience lack that puts you in financial bondage. If you do not already follow a focused financial plan you need the following principles and plan. You also need to stop listening to sources that tell you everyone is different and thus no specific plan works for everyone. This kind of belief will lead you to forsake adherence to any specific plan because you feel like you could never be sure it is one that works for you. Such talk is sheer nonsense. How many quality cars would be built if car manufacturers let every employee decide how they wanted to install parts, nuts, and bolts on vehicle frames as they moved down the assembly line? I doubt what is supposed to be the same model would look alike or would be of quality construction. If we are all different and would supposedly need a different plan to follow, would you let a brain surgeon perform a brain tumor removal if he did not have precise training and steps on how to remove tumors and a specific process from which to operate. I really doubt it!

Every person has the same body parts and organs and in the same locations. We are not so different as to eliminate the need for surgical plans or other plans that have been known to work for many other people who employed them. While we continue to educate ourselves going forward and thus may allow our surgeon and other practitioners to use some creativity with regard to new or revised methods if they intuitively make sense and research shows they work well, we see the best results for customers and people who use practices and processes that already have been proven to work. The main point here is, stop being immobilized by arguments that make no sense.

No man can claim to be so different that he does not need to worship, praise, pray, study scripture, fellowship with a local Church of believers, and serve others *(minister)* in ways that honor the LORD. Though we are unique in many ways and each person may have a different type of work to which they are called, biblical instruction applies equally to every person in the same manner. Those who want blessing & reward from Almighty God will be transformed by the renewing of their minds and thus conformed to His image *(living life and carrying out our work according to His instructions)*. The following weapons of spiritual warfare are needed for the financial realm of our lives to build the character and habits in us that our LORD desires to help us carry out His purpose: The Great Commandment & Commission placed on our individual lives and the Church.

CHAPTER 1

ELEVEN BIBLICAL PRINCIPLES FOR FINANCIAL FREEDOM & WEALTH BUILDING

Scripture teaches that good stewards engage in the following practices and they reap blessings from doing so:

PRINCIPLE 1: The LORD owns everything.
Revelation 4:11, Psalm 50:10-12, 1Chronicles 29:11

Manage money and resources like Almighty God owns it all because He does. In order to know His will for His money and resources you should regularly engage thanksgiving, praise, worship, and prayer. Also, write down a vision for your life and the management of money He entrusts to you based on what you understand His desire to be. Now, regularly declare and proclaim His will according to the vision the bible and His Spirit helped you formulate. This will help you engage in vision casting which encourages and motivates you to move forward pursing His design for your life, career, work, ministry, income, and resources.

It is necessary in order for you to truly understand and act upon the belief that He owns everything and that you're just a steward of what He owns who should be committed to managing it in the way that pleases Him. Understand that He owns everything ever created and thus has the right to decide its purpose and direct its use. Be wise in acting this out by making sure that everything you do is pleasing to Him and every resource you receive is used to serve others, your family, and yourself according to His will. Then your assets will truly have worth.

Learn to properly manage what He gives you to get the most out of it and to be found faithful to receive more to manage on His behalf, instead of doing everything humanly possible to get more money, fame, or power. Pursue your passion to serve the LORD and use the gifts He's given and skills you've developed in the marketplace to be the best manager you can be.

Such contentment will allow you to seek and be led by the Holy Spirit. A prayerful intimacy and action will move Him to supernaturally promote you to worthwhile positions and endeavors that immensely prosper you to achieve your life's purpose on earth as a result of your natural and humble work ethic. The truth of the scriptures shows a person who is faithful over little will be faithful over much and the Father loves to reward such faith-filled stewards.

Living by such faith is better than seeking the world's ideals of success and using its pathways based solely on human endeavor. Worldly methods are usually greed or poverty inspired temptations that seek to move you outside of His will to pursue things you feel are necessary to satisfy your fleshly longings or mindset instead of listening for the Holy Spirit to direct you to the things that please Him in order to fulfill your spiritual longings, true needs, and the needs of other people.

Such discontent always leads to greater heartaches and headaches because your desire to be fulfilled can never be satisfied by worldly riches, status, material things, or a poverty mindset. When the worldly, humanistic path is chosen, you do not allow His power to work to give you spiritual, eternal victory over troubles and obstacles that you will inevitably face. So, allow Him to create supernatural fulfillment and great success through contentment, according to His plan for your life.

Many people are not confident in their ability to be all He wants them to be. For some, this insecurity comes from feeling they're not worthy for Him to use or bless them. Others feel they're simply not good at math or planning. Still others believe they have not been elevated to an income level that really matters to Him.

Unfortunately, many people have been socialized to believe they are nobody unless they have a large income or an important title, authority, or fame. Many people express this view of themselves in their words and actions and some don't even recognize it. They say things about themselves or the position they are currently in that belittles them. Overtime, this produces great unconscious insecurity within them that will stop them from standing up, speaking out, or taking control in the ways they really need to throughout life.

The following and similar statements are signs of such insecurity, "I'm just a secretary" or "my opinion really doesn't matter" or "I'll never be anything good" or "I just can't manage money." The ideology behind such statements is satanically inspired because it is the opposite of what you should be saying, "I can do all things through Christ who strengthens me!" *(Philippians 4:13)*

Satan tries to blind the minds of all men to the truth, because he knows the truth will make you free. We can take the blinders off men by letting them know they are wonderfully made by Him with power to do everything He commanded them to do when they allow the Holy Spirit to lead them. Then by scripture and example, we can encourage them to love others, perform good works, and properly manage money for the benefit of His Kingdom, their families, and other people.

There's nothing wrong with having an important title and large income when your life is sanctified for His use. Yet everything is wrong with these things when the fruit thereof does not directly or indirectly honor Him, lead others to Him, and build them up in the faith. Every believer can perform mission's ministry no matter his/her position because he/she is an offspring of the Most High God.

Those that desire His kingdom to come and His will to be done will be used mightily to do the work of the ministry. They will spend time daily with the LORD in prayer and bible reading. In addition, they will tithe, give offerings, and use their physical and intellectual gifts to serve inside and outside their local Church. Honoring the LORD in these ways is where your turn-a-round starts and your trustworthiness is maintained.

Don't put all your effort in accumulating money and goods for earthly purposes. They decay, lose value, and have no eternal worth. Rather, build treasure in Heaven by giving abundantly to spread the gospel and make disciples for the LORD. The value of this treasure increases throughout eternity and where your treasure is your heart will be also.

His highest desire is that you seek a more intimate relationship with Him. Through this fellowship He is likely to provide you with many material blessings. Bible accounts of patriarchs / matriarchs with great wealth clearly show their wealth came from intimacy with Him and obedience to His will.

Earthly assets have eternal value only when they are used to spread the gospel and build the His kingdom in the hearts of men. So, take your cue from these leaders. Engage an intimate relationship with Jesus Christ. Understand that He owns everything ever created and thus has the right to decide its purpose and direct its use. Be wise in acting this out by making sure everything you do is pleasing to Him and every resource you receive is used to serve others, your family, and yourself according to His will.

Scripture tells us that Christians should be led by the Holy Spirit who lives in them. He will lead us to Jesus Christ, His will, and His way of being and doing things. In other words, in Christ your life will have the balance that is ordered for you to accomplish the things you need in accordance with scriptural principles.

Christ's balance will look unbalanced to some people and they may express negative comments about His way of doing things. However, when you are not balanced according to His calling, your life is ripe for destruction initiated by satan and brought about by ungodly morals and the actions produced by them. People who get off the LORD's narrow path usually fall into one of two financial extremes:

1. Stinginess, which is displayed by failing to faithfully support gospel work in the earth through their local Church, evangelistic, and discipleship ministries.
2. Materialism, which is displayed by the selfishness of spending beyond reason on things for themselves, thinking he who has the most toys wins the game, and not adequately preparing for rainy seasons in proportion to the money entrusted to them.

They wrongly think that money provides the protection and security they need. Also, they think they will miss something in life if they don't spend all their income and credit getting material things to appease their flesh and impress others. These mindsets are unproductive for your future and allow problems to overtake you at some point in your life. In addition, they fail to display the kind of trust you need to have in His grace to help you be and do everything you are called to do.

Only God in Christ can provide truly valuable eternal and earthly blessings. Failing to use godly stewardship to manage the money entrusted to you, which includes saving and investing, will put you in an uncomfortable position because catastrophic and emergency situations will arise throughout your life. These situations will require money and resources to alleviate.

Don't succumb to the two extremes that result from falling off of His path for you. Instead, allow Him to instill the proper balance for life and money management. From this pathway, you will do the things that will help you proceed and succeed throughout your life such as faithfully tithing, give offerings, caring for your family, and filling your life with fellowship and ministry with Him and the Church.

Jesus Christ's will and way are for His Church to love all people even though we may not like their attitudes or what they do. Sometimes you should not love your own attitudes and actions, yet even then He still loves you as a person and you should still love you. How much more then should you extend His mercy and grace to other people? The answer is always.

Thus, by the power of the Holy Spirit through faith, we work to spread the gospel in our families, communities, and around the world using words and deeds. The bible tells us that the foolishness of preaching the gospel one-on-one or to a congregation brings people of every race, creed, or nationality to Jesus Christ. It also lets us know that our nature was created in Him to do good works. Our stewardship of money plays an important role in expanding our reach. Over time, it enlarges our relationship building with people we come into contact with because it adds great force and effect to our words and deeds.

One important area of your witness is your desire and discipline in properly managing money entrusted to you. Everything you have comes from Him and your position in life would not be possible without His intervention and favor in your life.

People want to know that Jesus Christ made a tremendous difference in your finances because this is one of the foremost areas in which many are in bondage. Conversations that help them understand how to eliminate bondage can be a road that leads them to Christ. While you don't have the power to make them choose salvation and produce good fruit in their lives, you do have the ability to tell the truth in love about:

1. Eternal consequence of not accepting Jesus Christ as Savior and LORD;

2. Ignorance of and rebellion against biblical instruction that causes people to dwell in a dry land;
3. Financial habits and mismanagement that is destroying their earthly purpose;
4. His faithfulness in this life and throughout eternity in bringing His people victory over every temptation, trial, and obstacle they face.

Answer the call. In humility, seasoned by His grace, extending mercy, tell others the truth in love and do not forget that your management of money plays a tremendous role in your effectiveness and reach. You can make a tremendous difference for good in many other people's lives.

PRINCIPLE 2: Work diligently to be fruitful and produce income.

Genesis 2:15, Ephesians 4:27-28, 2Thessalonians 3:6-11

From everlasting, the LORD worked to create everything and set the spiritual and natural realm in motion. Then, He commanded man to work in order to be fruitful; cultivate the soil, raise animals, and engage physical and mental labor in many ways. Adam and Eve's worship, including their work, was totally enjoyable. After man chose to sin, he and his seed would eat by the sweat of his brow. Though work would still be enjoyable in many ways the deteriorating conditions that sin caused man to live in on earth would seem to make work more physically and mentally demanding, and in some instances unpleasant.

From the time that Adam disobeyed His command, the perfect communion they had was broken for all mankind. In sin, man sometimes chose work not meant for him. Though he might sometimes choose work for which he is gifted, he might also have unclean motives, attitudes, and actions or utilize the fruit thereof for ungodly purposes.

There is a truth about work that remains constant from the perfect beginning until now and into the saints' everlasting future; a person will always be fulfilled and thus have peace and joy when working as unto the LORD in every respect. Scripture confirms the diligent person will have everything needed to complete his / her purpose on earth and an able-bodied person who is lazy and irresponsible will not have what is necessary for fulfillment or comfort on earth!

There is an abundance of scripture confirming you should engage work *(both physical and mental)* for as long as you live. Total abstinence from work is not healthy for your body and mind. Lack of challenging work and daily regimen can bring about sickness, mental illness, and premature death. Therefore, He gives you work to accomplish throughout the course of your life: physical labor *(for producing income, wealth, and abundant giving)*, vocal and lifestyle worship, praise, prayer, bible and vocational study, various forms of service to believers and unbelievers, fellowship & hospitality, exercise, etc.

Also, there is an abundance of scripture telling you to stay away from lazy, idle, and irresponsible attitudes and behavior at all stages of life. Yet, godliness does not prohibit you from moving from one type of work to another as need or ability arises, unless you would engage in a type that is unholy according to scripture or that violates His will directly spoke to you. You are not prohibited from taking retirement from a current employer or business as long as you are mindful that you should engage reasonable work in another capacity. All types of work are worship and godly service *(ministry)* when they are committed to the LORD and engaged with His purpose in mind.

A necessary step to reversing your negative financial condition is to change your attitude about your current job. This applies whether you're self-employed or working for someone else. Begin to thank

Him for the work that is currently a blessing to you by providing an income you can use to take care of yourself, family, and other responsibilities.

No matter how small your paycheck appears to be, no matter how insignificant your position appears to be, and no matter how bad the atmosphere at work appears to be, you must thank Him for grace currently extended while you look forward to, envision, and set goals to capture future work opportunities along with greater income and employment relationships and situations that allow you to exercise your God-given gifts, skills, abilities, and purpose.

All experiences, whether good or bad, work together for your good because the LORD said so in His word. Your present situation will become a link to the next higher step in your career development when you become a diligent worker who does not murmur, who seeks to glorify Him by performing to the best of your ability, and who asks the Holy Spirit to help you find reasonable solutions to problem issues.

When you truly believe your work, employer, and/or entrepreneurial endeavors are blessings from Him and a step on the ladder that helps you fulfill His mission for your life and the Church, you oil the godly networking machine that positively changes your financial fortune. He is sure to show you how to stretch the income you receive and will increase it at various points in the future through promotions and new employment opportunities so you can do even more to reflect His glory in the earth and lead people to Him.

Don't become a lazy freeloader by relying on other people to provide for you at no cost. You must do the daily things you need to do to survive, live comfortably, and make a positive impact on others in this world. Slothfulness will cost you more lost money than not recognizing where your skills end and someone else's begin.

He wants to bless you immensely, rebuke the devourer, and stop satanic forces from causing you many spiritual and financial hardships. This comes only when you consistently work as unto the LORD and pay tithes and give offerings from your produce. This obedience is a necessary extension of faith that enables you to grow in holy and productive character. In this you display New Testament saving and sanctifying faith instead of empty words with no godly action behind them.

Faith without corresponding action is dead because it doesn't move you closer to His will. When you don't obey Him by allowing biblical principles to guide your life, you become a servant to Satan, sin, and those you borrow from. Your life, purpose, and worth will be on a path of destruction that will hinder your ability to live godly, minister to others, and prosper on earth. If left unchanged, this will lead to the destruction of your eternal relationship with Christ and the heavenly home He wants you to have.

Excellent, faithful work *(a job well done)* should be appreciated via promotions *(i.e., generous raises, higher level positions, accolades, awards, etc.)*. However, your employer and other people will fail to recognize your worth at different times during your life. Thus, there are times you may not receive a raise, promotion, or even an attaboy when you deserve it. The fact that you didn't receive some type of promotion is an opportunity for you to display great humility, patience, and love toward those who may have wronged you. You can only display this attitude of heart when you believe the LORD is the author and finisher of your faith and life who will open doors of promotion specifically for you when you're ready spiritually, mentally, emotionally, and physically to handle the new level of responsibility.

In the meantime, in between time, and when you get the promotion, use biblical financial principles such as working hard, respecting authorities that supervise you, and completing assignments well and on time in order to help others see it is in everyone's best interest to make other opportunities and responsibilities available to you. This attitude and course of action helps you build treasures on earth and in Heaven, as He helps you gain access to money and resources needed to complete steps toward your destiny.

Almighty God is totally reliable and has the master plan for your life. When you use His plan it additionally generates more peace, joy, and right-standing from which to receive even greater blessing. You must recognize this building block and order your life in such a way that you utilize it to move you ever forward. In the financial arena, biblical money management principles are what make up His plan.

Sometimes, people have been promoted but fail to recognize their promotion because it didn't seem to show up in the form of more money or a more prestigious title. However, He is also able to promote you by causing people to give you things free you otherwise would have to pay for. He also can cause events to take place that can reduce your expenses. These scenarios give you more disposable income to give for ministry and care for your family. Everyone committed to working as unto the LORD throughout life will see numerous promotions over time. So, don't let satan blind you to the reality of your promotions and don't be envious of promotions that others receive. Keep working effectively and He is sure to order your promotions from His throne when the time is right.

Old Testament scripture identifies that Levites were to retire from work at the temple when they turned fifty. They could continue to assist to a minor degree. There was no indication scripturally that this scenario applied to other professions. The New Testament indicates every Christian should continue *(until his / her last breath)* to evangelize, make disciples, and serve others. You may retire from a particular employer or type of work but you should continue working in at least a ministry capacity for the rest of your life.

Unless you want to retire into poverty, you need to employ appropriate financial management tools and processes that help you build an investment portfolio from which you can monthly *(for the remainder of your life)* withdraw enough money after taxes to cover all needs and at least some desires.

People whose employers provide pensions need not invest as much as those who work for employers that do not provide them. Those eligible to receive Social Security need not invest as much as those who are not eligible for it. People with both do not need to invest as much as those who only have one or the other. Those who have neither pension or Social Security obviously need to invest more than the others because investment income alone would have to cover the entire amount of all their expenses and desires during retirement.

The bottom line is everyone needs to invest a reasonable portion of their income *(start with 10%)* during working years in vehicles whose historical data prove they provide above average growth *(no-load low-expense total stock market index mutual funds, etc.).* In retirement, everyone will need to employ a good investment income withdrawal strategy that will last until they leave this Earth. This makes a comfortable, ministry-oriented, well-lived retirement possible.

There is hope if you find yourself in a poor financial situation right now. But you must understand life does not just arrange itself to provide what you need and want without you planning *(for some reasonable amount of time)* the earning and expending of income. From this point forward, you must budget, set aside emergency funds, eliminate debt, learn to live debt-free, invest, and give in ways that bring supernatural favor. The sooner you start the sooner you will be in position to comfortably retire and meet all expenses thereafter.

PRINCIPLE 3: Show contentment.
Luke 3:14, Philippians 4:11, 1Timothy 6:8

Continue or start tithing to your local Church or a worthwhile ministry each time you receive income. Choose delayed gratification instead of instant gratification. Do not buy that bigger house, more expensive car, new furniture, new jewelry, etc. until you have reached the priority goal of being a faithful tithing member of a local Church and totally debt-free. Stuff to buy will still be there at prices you can afford to pay after you reach your goal.

To grow spiritually, you must be content with the financial situation He placed you in. This doesn't mean you lack ambition to do more than you're now doing, rather it recognizes your appreciation for the present blessings that He's given you, that you consider closer fellowship with Him to be the success you seek, and that you wait on Him to open doors that lead you step-by-step to the fulfillment of your purpose and calling in Christ.

You must understand that what you consider to be the path leading to success may not be the path that the LORD wants you to choose. The blessings that come on His path for you far exceed what you believe you will get from the path you would choose. You must learn to hear His direction and options for your life. These can be heard only through prayer, reading the word, living by the word, and fellowshipping with the saints.

These disciplines should motivate you to use the following biblical financial principles to manage your current and future income:

1. Working regularly and diligently, including overtime and second jobs when you need more money to more quickly pay off debts. During periods of unemployment this means volunteering your time to worthy causes when you're not beating the street looking for income-producing work. When you don't have a job, you must look for work like it is your job with diligence and determination every day until you land one.

2. Budgeting diligently prior to and through each month to ensure what you are spending is less than your disposable income *(gross pay after taxes and other automatic deductions)*. You can trust the LORD to provide what you need *(through other people, organizations, etc.)* when you don't have money to pay for it.

3. Tithing each pay period.

4. Building an emergency reserve account of at least $1,000.

5. Using excess disposable income to pay off current debt. Also, refusing to continue using credit / debt to finance desires.

6. After all non-mortgage debt is eliminated, increasing the emergency fund to at least $10,000. Then, investing all disposable income into no-load low-expense stock index mutual funds.

When you delight yourself in Him by loving Him enough to do what He instructed, you'll receive the desires of your heart because the closer you get to Him the more His desires for you and mankind permeate your life and become your desires. You'll then have contentment by giving and building wealth from your present income source until you're promoted to a greater position of service to other people through entrepreneurship or your employer.

Being content is an attitude of heart and mind that will help you be a good steward of the resources and money He entrusts to you throughout the stages of your life. It is necessary in order for you to truly understand and act upon the belief that Almighty God owns everything and you're just a steward who should be committed to managing it in the way that pleases Him.

Contentment is necessary for you to recognize that tithing and giving offerings should be the first and foremost financial commitment in your budget *(giving saving spending plan)* because He commands His people to worship and serve Him in this manner. Contentment is necessary because this virtue helps you refuse to buy everything your eyes, flesh, and pride desire. It also helps you refuse to obtain loans to get even more than the cash flow from your income could provide.

It is an attitude of heart and mind, developed by the Holy Spirit, that does not leave you lacking. Rather, it leads you to the Rock that is higher than you, what you have, and what you can do. It helps you see the importance of developing an intimate relationship with Him that will help you engage every biblical principle you need to fulfill His purpose for you within His great plan for His people.

This direct pursuit of Jesus Christ leads indirectly to the prosperity He designed for your life and family.

By delighting yourself in Him, you draw closer to Him in fellowship and bypass the natural and eternal destruction brought about by succumbing to satanic temptation to gravitate to ungodly things that seem to glitter. As your fellowship with Him increases, the work you're ultimately called to on earth becomes more evident. You'll be motivated to use talents, spiritual gifts, and learned skills to bring about Christ's rule in the hearts of men.

You'll have a firm resolve to bypass the great amounts of money, fame, and power that you might possibly obtain by going down a path opposed to His will, because you understand that all future needs and desires He has for you will be met as you pursue your calling to glorify Jesus Christ, evangelize unbelievers, and equip believers.

As you find contentment in what's important to Him instead of what's important to you or other people, He will allow your career and ministry to others to take on much greater proportions than you thought possible. This humble and contrite attitude of heart and mind helps you properly manage money and resources and creates enormous future opportunities for you.

Instead of doing everything humanly possible to get more money, fame, or power, learn to properly manage what He has already given you in order to get the most out of it so you can be found faithful to receive more to manage on His behalf. Pursue your passion to serve the LORD and use the gifts He's given and skills you've developed in the marketplace to be the best work and income manager you can be – making widgets, providing service, and engaging financial disciplines as unto Him, the true rewarder of your efforts. Such contentment will allow you to seek and be led by the Holy Spirit.

PRINCIPLE 4: Sacrifice to initiate God's plan for work, ministry, and blessing.
Romans 12:1, Philippians 4:18, Hebrews 11:4

Sacrifice short-term pleasure for long-term financial soundness. Delayed gratification now *(because you need to employ it)* results in great benefits accruing to you in the long-run. It helps you receive the benefits of following biblical principles.

In order to have a solid spiritual foundation, you must believe with all your heart that He loves people so much that He sent His son Jesus Christ to die on the cross to eliminate the judgment due your sins in order that you, believing on Him, will have everlasting life. He loves you immensely and desires that you would choose to have relationship and fellowship with Him thru Christ even though you deserve eternal punishment for the sins you've committed throughout your life. He already provided the blood sacrifice and every spiritual tool necessary to secure your eternal life and blessing when you display faith in Jesus Christ. Sacrifice your own desires so you can please the LORD and faithfully endure hardship when needed to bring about His will in the earth, through good stewardship of the money and resources He entrusts to you.

The Holy Spirit living in you and guiding you as a result of your relationship with Christ enables you to forsake sinful, worldly ways of living via a continual maturity process *(sanctification and commissioning to good works in service to Him and people on earth)*. The first and greatest commandment leads believers to love Jesus Christ above all people and things and the second commandment leads us to love everyone else like we love ourselves. These are the foundation that must undergird all He called you to be and do.

This means you must manage your life, including your finances, in the way He identified in the bible; loving Him so much that you care more about spending money on earth in a manner that brings people to Him and builds treasure in Heaven, than you care about how much you can increase your material lifestyle and comfort.

This love leads to daily prayer and scripture reading which hides the Word in your heart. It also leads to regular weekly fellowship with other believers so you can move on to deeper fellowship with Him. These love-based disciplines constantly and faithfully aim you in the direction of engaging in biblically based good stewardship of your income, assets, and resources. This in turn ensures that you fulfill your God-given purpose and ministry calling to be blessed in order to be a blessing to many others.

Each of these methods requires you to become and remain disciplined in spending and saving in order for them to work to benefit you. They are not for the faint of heart, rather they are for those who are resolute in their desire to be godly stewards of money and become debt-free. Such people are willing to make necessary sacrifices to reach this financial position. They will engage biblical financial principles such as tracking income and expenses, cutting spending, reading financial literature to learn more about how to properly manage, honoring Him by giving to help spread the gospel and help others, and saving and investing for rainy days and future purposes.

He will help you increase in each of these areas while helping you maintain a heart of humility and sacrifice for His kingdom and the sake of other people. This will allow you to be a much greater blessing to your local Church, your community, and missions work around the world. Be willing to sacrifice by not worrying about or trying to purchase items you cannot pay for at the current time even though you believe you need or desire them. This displays trust in Him and allows Him to provide for you and your family when you cannot. You will find that many things you consider a need are not really a need and that you can wait on desires until you are able to purchase them without the burden of debt and the negative consequences that follow it. This lifestyle of utilizing biblical principles presents your body as a living sacrifice that is holy and acceptable to Him.

Getting yourself in debt, failing to tithe, and spending more than your net-income are ways in which you dishonor Him. Not to mention, you dishonor yourself because you're not operating in accordance with who He made you to be: *(a)* one who shows love by following His commands; *(b)* an abundant giver instead of one looking to give the least he can; *(c)* a leader who is an example for others to follow. Don't be led by the blind, who twist bible verses to suit their selfish aims. Be a person willing to sacrifice comfort in order to see Christ formed in yourself and other people!

It's natural for hard work at a legitimate job or business to prosper you over the long haul through raises, promotions, greater opportunities, and good management of your income. This situation provides for increased comforts and flexibility throughout your life. Yet, in order to know whether or not you have a proper perspective on prospering and being successful, you should continually ask will I still claim Jesus Christ as Savior and LORD, manage my life by His principles, give up anything that does not help me grow in Christlikeness, and focus on Him and what He called me to be and do when things get real tight or my income is drastically reduced or I need to reduce expenses in the short-term in order to move forward into long-term financial health and vitality?

I certainly hope your answer is LORD as we move into the future, I am ready, willing, and able to sacrifice things, positions, and notoriety in order to be blessed and rewarded by You so I can be a blessing to many others.

Being faithful often requires that you sacrifice some pleasures early on to reduce the amount you would otherwise pay creditors *(i.e., reducing spending on personal pleasures in order to prioritize tithes and offerings to the LORD)*. This results in His supernatural blessing on your finances by getting the devil off your case so He does not devour the seed and bread given to you and stop you from being fruitful in the future. It also keeps Heaven's windows open for greater opportunities for you in endeavors and arenas in which you can exhibit Christlikeness in your conversation and conduct, giving glory to Him.

Exercising self-control and being willing to sacrifice current pleasures is also on His heart so you consistently spend far less than the income you make and also save a meaningful portion of your income in order to repel the clutches of materialism and be aware that some things he is calling you to do and situations you will face will require the use of increased assets in the future. Many people find that inexplicable promotions, bonuses, and greater income producing opportunities come their way after they consistently employ the principles of stewardship, abundant giving, sacrifice, contentment, and self-control that lead to the use of other principles like debt-elimination, no cosigning, saving & investing, and diversifying assets. They begin to understand that this process is not a pledge of poverty or acceptance of lack, rather it is one that trusts the LORD to provide His very valuable treasures designed for them in due time in the way that is pleasing to Him and most beneficial to them and to those to whom they are to be godly examples.

Be patient recognizing over time this level of faithfulness will positively bless you, your family, and other people by providing ever-increasing money and resources to meet needs and enjoy meaningful desires. Do not be like people who become weary in well doing and give up right before the ultimate blessing, anointing, and inheritance rains upon them. Even if your earthly destiny ends in martyrdom, you will immediately receive eternal treasure, joy, and stature becoming of the sacrifice in glorifying Jesus Christ and helping build His kingdom. The prosperity portal from Heaven to earth is very important because it allows you to gain wealth, be rich in good works, generous, and always ready to serve. It should lead you to use, in a God-honoring way, anything He entrusts to you.

Develop a bare bones budget *(income and spending plan)* that helps you identify the amount of money needed to pursue your calling and vision *(career and ministry)*. Be willing to sacrifice enjoyments in the short-term *(no desire should be a sacred cow that cannot be eliminated)* in order to make it through training and develop the skills and learn of tools that can make you valuable and provide higher income. Of course, the first and foremost priority should be to have an intimate born again relationship with Jesus Christ and learn His ways and standards. Seek to employ the evangelism and disciple-making power He placed in you in the calling / career field selected by confirmation of and laying on of hands of the presbytery, so you can be right in the center of His will as your forge out into the work-a-day world for the rest of your life.

It's important to be humble so you don't require the pastor, elders, leaders, or other members to recognize your contributions - know the LORD recognizes your faithful service to others that glorifies Him. He ultimately causes your faithfulness to rise from obscurity in His timing, not yours, so that leaders and others somewhere within the body of Christ and most times within your local fellowship begin to recognize your commitment, obedience, and sacrifice.

This is His process for increasing your wisdom and stature with Him and man. This process creates steps for you to rise to elevated platforms of ministry / leadership within and outside the Church walls that give you a greater audience to whom you can minister in a way that gives Him glory. Your resolution should be so strong that you are willing to crucify your own will wherever it will impede His will from taking place in your life and ministry.

When you have not specifically heard what He uniquely desires as your specific life calling, you must follow the vision and goals set by Him for His Church, as identified in scripture *(worship, evangelism, disciple-making, and serving others)*. Also, you must be ready for Him at any time to identify more of His vision for your life as well as goals to move you ever closer to fulfilling the vision. The greatest fulfillment and rewards are reserved for people who consistently engage faith through actions that please Him.

Being a good steward of the manifold blessings, He provides demands that you start right where you are in your relationship with Jesus Christ as Savior & LORD of your life. Understand that presenting your body as a living sacrifice, holy and acceptable to Him, and being transformed by the renewing of your mind means you must follow biblical principles as soon as you learn them because they serve as the gateway to truly doing His will. Your intimate relationship with the true and living God and where you truly stand in readiness to do His will are verified when you adhere to principles such as worshipping Him via thanksgiving, praise, prayer, daily bible study, weekly fellowship with believers, and making godly declarations / proclamations of your fruitfulness & prosperity. Likewise, your godly example is magnified when you employ the few principles aimed primarily at the financial area of your life: tithing, offering, planning including budgeting, debt elimination, refusing to cosign, saving & investing, and diversifying your investments.

Whether you are a business owner, executive, politician, manager, or employee refuse to think more highly of yourself than you do of other people. Always refuse to oppress people, do not work them like slaves, and pay them fair wages based on godly standards, because it is in your power to do so and it ultimately blesses you as much as them and their immediate family. When sacrifices need to be made you should make deep and sometimes greater sacrifices than you ask of those under your authority. These are ways in which you love your neighbor as yourself and thus bring God-pleasing fruitfulness and reward into your life and ministry.

So, as you pursue money making, managing, investing, and business pursuits make sure you maintain your love relationship with the LORD, spend time with Him daily, be guided by His Spirit, obey His biblical commands and principles, and speak and act as Christ's ambassador on the earth. Take instruction from the examples of missionaries we love so much and support. His love in them and trust in His care compels them to move into hostile territory, to face possible death, and to endure suffering.

Tens of millions of dollars flow into their hands, yet they do not put their trust in it. Rather, they recognize they are blessed to be a blessing to many others. Love moves them to sacrifice, suffer afflictions, and great personal loss at times on earth to spread this great gospel throughout the world. They shall receive an everlasting crown from Him that is much more precious and enduring. This too should be your focus as you sacrifice short-term pleasure for long-term and eternal gain.

PRINCIPLE 5: Show self-control.
Proverbs 25:28, 1Corinthians 7:5, 9:25, Galatians 5:22-23

This is a fruit of the Spirit mentioned in Galatians 5. Along with the other eight fruit it shows you walk in the Spirit and not according to the flesh. Pleasing the LORD is the ultimate goal anyone can have and this goal can only be displayed by living according to His commands. You must learn to be obedient to biblical principles in order to control your fleshly appetite and focus on fulfilling His purpose for your life. This will help produce wealth in a way pleasing to Him.

Satan employs a major strategy of introducing you to ideas that put the greatest priority in life on earning great amounts of money, stockpiling wealth beyond reason, seeking success and high profile among men, and pursuing material pleasures in ways that diminish your ability to fellowship with the LORD. His demonic cohorts constantly bombard you with such ideas through media articles, infomercials, internet spam, person to person communication, and some pulpits.

They know loving money is the root of all evil and covetousness and idolatry are able to eternally destroy your life. When they can convince you that it is better to spend your time trying to get rich, they diminish your desire to learn truth by fellowshipping with Him in prayer and bible study.

Their age-old strategy includes trying to convince you He is okay with any activity or business endeavor that makes lots of money. They try to convince you the LORD rejoices when you spend all your time working to obtain more money and situations that might bring you power, fame, and notoriety on earth. Such mistaken beliefs have caused many divorces, neglected children, oppression in the workforce, and eternal separation from Him for those unrepentant prior to death who did not make Christ's will their priority. This is not His best for you!

Faithfully maintaining daily devotions, fellowship with believers, and managing your activities and finances according to biblical principles eliminates such problems and produces everything you need for life and godliness on earth and stores treasures in Heaven that await you. It also produces an abundance of resources in your life far beyond most people's experience and it shows the priority upon which your heart is focused: for where your treasure is, there your heart will be also! *(Matthew 6:21)*

Throughout the existence of mankind, the LORD has instructed man on how to live trusting His fatherly character and grace to provide us with everything we need for life and godliness. He wants you to understand that anything needed beyond your level of current wealth should rely on Him and employing his economic principles. Being content helps you exhibit self-control to restrain your purchases and builds you into the humble, useful, and fruitful man or woman of God you are designed to be because it leads you to tithe to worthwhile Church ministries in order to build His kingdom in people's hearts through preaching, teaching, and good works.

It also leads you to budget with a plan to give abundantly, eliminate debt, save, invest, and diversify. This pattern brings supernatural blessing upon you that will remove the pressure of debt and allow a large portion of your income to be given for the work of ministry and fulfillment of your purpose. At a later stage in life, it allows you to afford more things you desire without going into debt to get them. This tends to happen only five to seven years after you purpose in your heart and take action to truly live out biblical financial principles.

How would you feel if this rich life applied to you? I'll tell you: you'd feel great about ever abounding in the work of the LORD and being a good example of Christian stewardship to everyone around you. So, get started today by committing to His way and changing those patterns in your life that are not in line with biblical instruction.

He loves you immensely and desires that you be close to Him even though you deserve eternal damnation based on the sins you've committed throughout your life. In Jesus Christ, He made a way for your eternal security and by the power of the Holy Spirit you can forsake sinful, worldly ways of living by engaging a continual maturity process.

In order to do so, you must recognize that love is the most essential part of being a disciple of Jesus Christ. You must believe with all of your heart God so loved the world that He gave His only begotten Son, that whoever believes in Him should not perish but have everlasting life *(John 3:16)*. You must love Jesus Christ above everyone and everything. This should lead you to manage your life, including your finances, in the way identified in the bible so you can be a good steward, Christ's witness, and His example to other people.

Loving Him leads you to daily pray and study scripture to hide His Word in your heart. It also leads you to exhibit the fruit of the spirit in your life and communication. The fruit of self-control is especially important in helping you manage the money He allows you to have. Without it you will not truly fulfill the purpose He has for your place in your family, ministry, vocation, or society. Loving people leads you to fellowship with other believers weekly. It helps you know you need what they provide and they need what you provide.

It is through loving Him and people *(in the manner described in the bible)* that you will have deeper fellowship with Him, better relationships with those around you, and move forward to be a good steward of your life and finances and fulfill your purpose, ministry, and vocational calling(s).

Many children are being left to raise themselves because parents are making other issues more important than spending quality time teaching principles that will make the children's lives more purposeful, meaningful, balanced, peaceful, and joyful, as they grow into adulthood.

A lot of parents are giving children the impression that:

1. It is important to have every material thing and career position you want and to be willing to pay any cost to get it.
2. Keeping up with the Joneses is the priority of life.
3. Being in debt is a great way to live and obtain all the comforts of life.
4. You should work as many hours as seems humanly possible to make as much money and gain as much notoriety as you can even if it means spending little time with the family *(in essence destroying the marriage and the family unit)*.

Most parents are not teaching biblical money management principles that will help their children be content, self-controlled, service-focused, and prosperous in life nor are they directing them to sources that could help them learn these valuable virtues and the methods that can help employ them.

Leading children to Jesus Christ should be the first priority of every parent and guardian. They should also be led to pursue His will for their lives and incomes and any money and resources that come into their hands.

This will not happen when the parent or guardian is not focused on pursuing His will. Children usually absorb what they see in parents and guardians more than they absorb what parents and guardians say and usually to a greater degree.

When the children see a continually ungodly example, many times they develop a greater addiction to it and bring greater destruction into their lives than the parents experienced. When they hear and see godly examples, the children have a much greater influence that keeps them in the Light that enables them to achieve greater levels of prosperity on earth than their parents achieved.

You will probably not teach the correct principles and lessons of life if you don't follow them yourself. Is your child's future important enough to make sure he / she inherits eternal life and has the tools to live prosperously on earth using money management principles that please Him?

Thank God there is hope even when parents have not taught or exampled the right lifestyle and money management principles and methods because the Holy Spirit never stops reaching out to people, including children, with the truth of eternity and of living in purpose and meaning here on earth. You simply do not want to be used as a tool of satan that serves as a stumbling block whose attitudes and actions lead your children, teens, young adults, and those you influence away from the Truth, biblical principles, faith in action, and good stewardship that lead to eternal and earthly prosperity.

Yet, you must also understand that exercising self-control and being willing to sacrifice current pleasures is also on His heart so you consistently spend far less than the income you make and also save and invest a meaningful portion of your income in order to repel the clutches of materialism and be aware that some things He is calling you to do and situations you face require the growth and use of such assets in the future.

Many people find that inexplicable promotions, bonuses, and greater income producing opportunities come their way after they consistently employ the principles of stewardship, abundant giving, sacrifice, contentment, and self-control that lead to the use of other principles like debt-elimination, no cosigning, saving & investing, and diversifying assets. They begin to understand the process is not a pledge of poverty or acceptance of lack, rather it is one that trusts the LORD to provide His very valuable treasures designed for them in due time in the way pleasing to Him and most beneficial to them and those they are to be a godly example to.

Accepting Jesus as your Savior and LORD and seeking His kingdom and righteousness is crucial, above all else, in order to rightly use the income, time, and talent He has given you. While daily reading the bible, you'll recognize the ways it shows you how to faithfully honor Him publicly and privately. He will supernaturally bless you beyond what you have envisioned as you pray daily, study the bible daily, give praise to Him throughout the day, listen for His instructions, fellowship weekly with other believers, pay tithes, give offerings, and regularly help a Church ministry perform its service. Pleasing Him is the ultimate desire you should have with a mind toward creating a place where His peace and joy in the Holy Ghost permeates your life in the natural and eternal realms. Then and only then will the bulk of your blessings and rewards have maximum usefulness for you and other people.

Only five to ten percent of all people are in good financial condition. This small group live content, self-controlled, and servant-minded with regard to others people's true need for Jesus Christ. They are committed to living constructively debt-free and managing money He entrusts to them in a way where they control expenses so they are continuously far less than their take home pay. They follow a simple budget so well that they have plenty of money left over throughout each year that can be applied to savings for emergencies and for big ticket items they will need or want in the future *(special offerings, different house or car, vacation, wedding ceremony, etc.)*. Each year, they are also able to put at least 10% of their gross pay into a diversified portfolio of equity investments that have proven track records over ten or more years of paying high average annual interest and/or exponential growth. They are grateful with much thanksgiving for the intimacy they share with the LORD and the Church family. They are reputable in their dealings, known for paying back what is owed to others, and for being a blessing in the lives of those around them.

Many of the other ninety to ninety-five percent of people often complain about their position in life, the jobs they hold, and their relationships with spouses and/or other people. They're up to their necks in debt, are often broke again shortly after getting paid, and continually buy more expensive houses, cars, boats, campers, cabins, and clothing above their income and asset level. They quickly replace these items with more expensive ones while paying lenders enormous amounts of down payment, closing costs, and finance charges over the term of the many loans they have outstanding. They act as if they cannot live without continually getting loans for everything they need and want.

Yet, many people wonder why their lives and finances are in shambles. Some have been taught that the LORD wants to pour more money and expensive material things into their lives but requires no accountability, responsibility, and discipline from them. Of course, this could not be further from the truth. Many have simply not studied to show themselves approved as workmen that need not be ashamed because they rightly understand the Word of Truth and all its instructions on good stewardship of their lives including money entrusted to them.

Despite this predicament, help is on the way when they decide to have faith in His way of living by exercising self-control. You can change your spiritual and financial situation from negative to positive when you leave the former way of doing things and begin to regularly worship the LORD by praying to Him, studying scripture, fellowshipping with Christians, using your gifts and skills in service to others, tithing, budgeting, eliminating debt, refusing to cosign, saving, investing, and diversifying. A whole new world awaits you, free of complaints about your current and future condition and full of testimonies to other people about your life full of His abundant mercy, grace, peace, joy, blessing, and reward.

PRINCIPLE 6: Tithe and give offerings.
Genesis 14:20, Malachi 3:8-12, Matthew 23:23, Hebrews 7:8

This honors the LORD for His provision and helps fund the spread of the gospel to every person around the world. When you are filled with the Holy Spirit you will seek to be a witness for Jesus Christ while on Earth. The Great Commission also points out that we are to disciple people – teach them about obedience to everything Jesus commanded. This principle helps us properly respond to the spiritual atmosphere He desired, which is developing intimacy with Him, evangelizing other people who do not yet know Him, and making disciples of them. Our giving to worthwhile ministries helps us do these things at home and abroad. When we cannot be there to do them in person, we provide funds for others to carry the gospel message of Jesus Christ.

We are often asked when should one start tithing and giving offerings. The answer is as soon as you have read the bible and understand the LORD instructed it, no matter your age. When you are adolescent, you will be given money *(by your parents, grandparents, aunt, uncles, etc.)* long before you work to earn money. This is income to you, therefore parents, preachers, and teachers should teach you to begin tithing and offering at the point of receiving money, so at an early age you set the spiritual atmosphere of displaying faith in Him, which entails showing obedience to his instruction, that you will follow for the remainder of your life. This produces continual harvests and rewards for your life that may not otherwise come to you *(gifts, bonuses, benefits, promotions, and the most important - knowledge that you are pleasing His heart and helping other people draw closer to Him).*

Failing to give the LORD the portion of your income He commanded traps you in a negative spiritual and/or financial condition. Frustration and heartache replace peace and joy when you do not honor Him before you spend the lion's share on yourself & give little to help other people. You should never want to be in the position of robbing Him of the proportion of income He provided you that scripture shows you should give for betterment of your family, Church, and you.

Often times people can look to this area of managing finances to identify that failing to tithe is allowing satan to keep them in financial bondage. Marital arguments over money, wondering why you don't have money to care for things you consider needs, and the inability to save money for future needs and have more than enough for long-term investing to grow wealth are only symptoms / results of financial mismanagement. They are not the source of the problem. Yet, you cannot correct the situation and be led out of financial bondage until you recognize the problem and deal with it by changing your habits to engage good money management principles including giving like the bible instructs.

The LORD allows you to have all the income you live on right now and all that you will ever have access to! If you do what He commands He promised to open Heaven's windows and pour out a blessing on you. It will be so much you will have to share His blessing with many others. In addition, He promised to rebuke the devourer for your sake so such evil spirits do not ruin your life or your finances and thus you can be fruitful in all you put your hand to do.

A tithe is one-tenth of your gross income. Offerings are free-will in nature and should be given cheerfully as you purpose in your heart to your local Church, other ministries, and the needy. When you give abundantly, the LORD will abundantly give to you so at all times you will receive more than enough to complete every good work He calls you to engage. He will bountifully provide for those who faithfully tithe and give offerings to support ministry work.

The bible warns everyone not to trust in money no matter what assets or income they hold in life because it will fail you. Thus, it will dishonor the LORD and display a lack of trust for you to withhold tithing and offering while spending that money upon yourself when you know it can help unbelievers hear the gospel and be led to Him and will help believers be matured into disciples. He designed our lives to enable us to live on far less than ninety percent of take-home income while we tithe and give offerings, pay government taxes, pay necessary household expenses, and *(within reason for our stage of life and income)* get some things we desire without going into debt. Unfortunately, many people unfaithful to His instructions find they cannot live on 100% of income He entrusts to them. Failing to follow scriptural commands results in many problems in your life that could have been avoided by doing things His way.

Only what you do for Jesus Christ will last. Through this relationship He is helping you build an eternal habitation in heaven and a portal on earth for other men to find Him and experience the depth of love that you've come to know. He provides lifestyle principles and some material things for the faithful *(rich and poor)* who adhere to His plan. This allow them to live at far less than the 90% of take-home pay while tithing and giving more of their income to their local Church and other ministries in order for the gospel to be spread worldwide and be a blessing to many others. He truly has blessed you with your current income and assets and everything you may receive in the future so you are blessed to be a blessing throughout the earth through funding ministries that you may or may not have an ability to work with physically.

The biblical model of money management recognizes that more money and more things will not make you happier or better, rather fulfilling His purpose for your life will bring fulfillment. Thus, the lifestyle that helps draw into your life the kind of people, resources, money, and other elements He will use to help you fulfill His plan for your life is the kind that meets your true needs and builds wealth that lasts throughout many generations and into eternity. For where your treasure is, there your heart will be also. *(Matthew 6:21)*

No matter the size of your income you can, in an abundant way, deliver the gospel of Christ to other people. The parable of the talents and minas in the books of Matthew and Luke show that He expects you to properly manage your talent, mind, income, and assets according to His commands. You can expect great blessings when you follow His instructions.

The opposite form of lifestyle and money management thinks the winner is the one with the most money, stuff, position, power, and earthly influence. This lifestyle brings eternal if not earthly destruction and fails to provide you and other loved ones with the

RANDY PARLOR

principles, fortitude, and activities necessary to be truly successful in His eyes.

He recognizes that you honor Him first when your heart is conditioned to budget your income so your plan is always to first make sure He will receive *(thru His Church – the local representation of Jesus Christ on earth)* the portion of your income that scripture instructs.

Tithing and offering to Him first may be possible when you're an entrepreneur who makes the decision how all disbursements from your gross business revenue will be given out. However, it is impossible for most people who work for employers obligated by Uncle Sam to automatically take income and payroll tax from their gross pay and forward it to federal, state, and local governments.

The fact that you cannot actually give to the LORD first is not dishonoring to Him in this situation because you cannot exert control over this government mandated process. He is more interested in you not giving Him blemished, spotted, wrinkled, and crippled sacrifices with regard to the after-tax income that is in your control. Again, spending first on all your desires and even things you feel you need when you have not set aside the tithe and an offering for Him and His kingdom use is dishonoring Him because it shows that you do not trust Him to care for all your need while you follow His instructions.

That house, car, kid's camp, private school tuition, food, clothing, etc. is not more important than following His commands and instructions. We must let our hearts be transformed in the area of managing income and giving in recognition that His every word is our necessary food. When you follow scriptural instructions, He will take care of all your need and many times way beyond that even if your current situation looks grim.

The scriptures about Abraham, Jacob, faithful Israelites as well as Jesus instructions in Matthew 23:23 and the example in Hebrews 7:8 show that the tithe given to Jesus' under-shepherd's on earth *(Church leaders)* are received by Him in Heaven and is the starting point for determining faithfulness managing our income to glorify Him. Beyond that He desires that we willingly give an offering because we love Him and other people and desire to see them reached with the gospel and saved from destruction.

The organism and mechanism He built for carrying out that mission is His organized Church lead by elders such as apostles, prophets, evangelists, pastors, and teachers who equip believers and administer all the physical aspects needed to make it happen *(meeting places, tools, classes, volunteers, paid staff, instruction to deacons, etc.)*. You are disorganized and in chaos spiritually *(and it may show itself in the natural)* when you fail to fellowship with a local Church He established, as shown in the scripture that He told us to regularly worship with and not forsake such assembly and to do so more and more because we know His return and Judgment Day are coming soon.

You've been asked by various charities to make a pledge to help them do the work they were formed to do or ministries have asked you to pledge money over and above your tithe and regular offerings, yet your budget does not show that you could give any extra money. At this point, the pressure is on because you always want to bless ministry work with an abundant offering, you don't want to be considered faithless, and you know there are always people you can help by spreading the gospel and meeting basic needs. So, what should you do?

This scenario is good reason for you to focus on spending less than you make, for pursuing a debt-free life, and for amassing assets to help others meet future needs because this lifestyle will afford you future opportunities to be a blessing to many others without placing yourself in the position of a poor steward. Before you pledge to anyone or any organization you should consult the bible to find out what it has to say about pledging, swearing, surety, and making oaths and you should ask the Holy Spirit what you should do.

If you decide to pledge without setting qualifiers on it, remember it is an oath to Him so pay it off when due because you love Him and don't want to dishonor His name. It's not a good idea to pledge from emotions, because it can lead to guilty feelings, legal obligations, callousness toward paying the pledge, or sinful methods to obtain the money, and broken relationships when you don't do what others expect you to.

The qualifier that you can set on sacrificial giving is to make it a "faith promise" in which you agree to give a certain amount of money when He releases to you that amount or greater over and above what your current income would provide. Make it clear in your heart that you will give it when received and ask Him to open Heaven's windows and show you ways to reasonably produce more income to bless and help others. Whether or not He provides the pathway for the "faith promise" funds and I believe He will, it is always best to consistently tithe and give abundant offerings to your local Church and selected ministries from your current income while prayerfully asking Him to increase your resources so you can give even more in the future.

It's interesting that most people give away far more money in interest and fees to financial institutions than they do to honor the LORD. It's also interesting that people on average give less than 2% of their income to the Church and promote the argument that He does not require anyone to tithe. This is their basis for giving whatever they decide to give or feel they can afford to give. Yet, they feel justified in spending far more than the tithe on unnecessary material desires that satisfy the lust of the flesh, lust of the eyes, and pride of life.

The Old Testament and The New Testament clearly show that tithing is a faith principle that blesses those who do not shut their mind and hands to it. It is a practice that helps improve our spiritual and natural well-being. It shows we love the LORD more than anything on this earth, including money. It also helps discipline us to live within our means and organize our stewardship of the resources He provides so we can build the structure of our lives and ministry in the marketplace according to His principles and not the rudiments of the world.

PRINCIPLE 7: Planning - tell your life and finances what to do.
Proverbs 27:23-27, Habakkuk 2:2-4, Luke 14:28-30

Live on less than your income by planning *(budgeting)* your giving, saving, and spending. Know the state of your flocks and herds and write the vision down plainly on paper so you can successfully use it to reach the desired goal.

You are committing financial suicide when:

- Your monthly income cannot cover all the bills you are supposed to pay each month.
- You're spending all your monthly income and do not have at least $1,000 in an emergency fund.
- You're applying for loans to get even more than you can afford to pay cash for.
- You're failing to immediately add deposits to your checkbook balance and to subtract the amount of each check written from your checkbook balance.
- You're failing to reconcile your bank account(s) monthly.

You're a kamikaze whose plane will inevitably hit a ship and burst into flames. The saddest part is you'll also hurt your spouse, children, other dependents, and your local Church by not being a good steward of money the LORD entrusts to you.

The bible instructs you to plan and keep records so you know the state of your income versus expenditures. You must consistently keep the amount of monthly household expenses below the amount of monthly take home pay in order to have financial peace and joy in your life. Some people don't like to hear the word budget. However, when you don't budget the reality is you inevitably overspend your income and thus get trapped in debt, lack of giving, and financial bondage. The word budget seems restrictive to some people because they think it limits control, pleasure, and stature derived from things purchased. However, when properly drafted, a budget shows what your income allows you to live on and what is necessary to have a healthy financial status. You will derive long-term joy and peace by eliminating debt, learning to live debt-free, and building wealth than you will by taking on more debt to get stuff and experiences. Happiness derived from the latter is very short-term in nature and costs you a bundle of future wealth you'll never get back.

If you don't like what the budget shows you concerning limitations inherent on your income level, then the budget has done its job by leading you in the right direction by showing you the need to use skills and abilities to initiate entrepreneurial endeavors and extra work to earn more money to maintain and increase giving, saving, and standard of living. In addition, it will have done a great job showing you the right-sizing and/or elimination of monthly expenses necessary to maintain financial integrity and soundness in your dealings until such time as you actually receive consistently increased income from your work efforts.

When your monthly outgo exceeds your monthly income, your upkeep will be your downfall! You must learn to consistently spend less than your income in order to *(a)* have a healthy financial life, *(b)* give abundantly, *(c)* accumulate necessary savings for rainy days, and *(d)* be in the wealthy place the LORD reserves for His sons and daughters. The budget or whatever you choose to call it *(giving / saving / spending plan, etc.)* shows you when spending exceeds income and allows you to employ simple math necessary to determine which expenses can be immediately right-sized or eliminated and how much increased income is needed to cover necessary bills and also to put an adequate amount toward outstanding debt so they can be eliminated within the next couple of years. Therefore, you must employ a budget you regularly consult and update to chart your financial path in a way that helps you get everything out of your income that will serve the LORD's purposes for your life, family, and involvement with the Church.

Your budget should be designed to ensure you *(a)* give an acceptable proportion of your income to gospel ministry for evangelism & disciple-making, *(b)* save and invest a proportion necessary to help you live comfortably when in your senior years, and *(c)* spend an appropriate portion to care for needs and engage some desires and pleasure early in life in a way that keeps you financially healthy. The road to financial health and wealth is not hard to find or stay on, but it takes diligence in applying tools like budgeting, debt elimination, saving, and investing to get where the LORD wants you to go. The diligent soul shall be prosperous because He rewards people who diligently seek Him by employing biblical financial principles in their lives.

When you spend all that you make and continually obtain loans and use credit cards to get everything you want, the day will come when you will have a mountain of bills you cannot pay. Some worldly pundits tout paying yourself first as the solution to all your financial problems. However, that method does not work, unless you know what your monthly net after-tax income and consistently spend less than that amount minus what you pay yourself first during the month. Otherwise, you will eventually stop paying yourself first and borrow it all back to obtain needed cash in order to pay creditors that have cajoled you into an unreasonable lifestyle given your current income.

Do not be fooled, whether you are considered rich or poor, you can get into a habit of spending more than your net income. The bible instructs you to write your vision down on paper, so you can remember it and take steps to achieve it with His supernatural guidance & power. You must craft a giving saving spending plan *(budget)* in order to maintain good financial health. It will help you achieve the vision and callings He places on your life.

Discipline yourself to write down your estimated

giving-saving-spending plan for each of the next six months. Then, be intentional on consulting it and following its pattern while refusing to ever again get caught in the borrowing/credit trap. This type of plan is a simple tool utilized to gauge monthly income versus expenditures so you can live within your means in a manner that allows you to take care of your top priorities and build wealth for the future.

First, write down your monthly net income from every source and total the figures. Then from that total subtract monthly tithes and offering and each of your anticipated expenditures *(food, shelter, transportation, utilities, loan payments, etc.)* based on your current obligations and spending. Tithing and offering should be the first category in the expenditure section of your budget because it honors the LORD for providing the means to care for yourself, family, and spread the gospel message. Next, account for payments for all necessities like rent, groceries, household utilities, etc. Next, subtract all other minimum payments such as car notes, credit card payments, mobile phone payments, etc.

Use all extra cash left over each month *(after all minimum payments have been accounted for)* to pay down your smallest total debt. When that creditor is completely paid off take all extra cash to pay down the creditor that is now owed the smallest amount until it is completely paid off. Continue this snowball pattern until all debt is completely eliminated. The snowball debt elimination method provides a psychological edge for people who need to see accounts paid off quicker in order to maintain focus and motivation to keep moving toward total debt freedom. For most people with focus and determination it will take less than a couple of years to complete this task for non-mortgage debt and it immediately begins to increase your net worth and help you build wealth that will grow abundantly over time. The LORD promised to supply all your need when you commit to His way of doing things.

Budgeting *(a Giving-Saving-Spending Plan)* is a financial principle of utmost importance necessary to help you prosper and build wealth to fulfill the callings the LORD places on your life. Write down the vision He inspires for your life taking into account your gifts, abilities, guidance from parents, words of prophecy, knowledge, and wisdom from other trustworthy, godly sources, and resources available to you and those you can seek *(which are many)*.

Identify where you see yourself in one year, five years, and ten years and adapt your budgetary aim toward that vision by *(a)* rightsizing expenses to eliminate any that will not help you expediently get to the place you envision and *(b)* pursuing no cost, low cost entrepreneurial endeavors that will produce greater income to get you there. Remembering your vision and keeping an eye on your budget several months in advance will quickly let you know how much disposable income you will have available and how much you can spend in current and future pay periods in pursuit of your goals. In addition, it will let you know the breadth of your vision that the LORD must supernaturally facilitate in order for you to meet your goals and destiny. Never hesitate to put the greatness of His vision for you before Him daily as you worship, give thanks, praise, and pray.

Intimacy with Him and consistently consulting His vision for your life will eliminate the urge to spend money on and get loans for material things that will not take you toward the stature He wants your life to represent. The Holy Spirit will help you plan for future activities and investment goals that take you there. A vision and budget are not hard to follow when you stay out of debt because as bill entries are eliminated, your disposable income *(cash flow)* grows enabling you to spend more on the resources necessary to fulfill the vision. Over time, His goals for you will come to pass and He'll give you more money and responsibility to manage for His glory.

Your wallet will contain holes and your life will be filled with embarrassment when you don't have an established ongoing vision and budget you consult before making spending decisions. However, money managed according to biblical principles blesses you and will also be used to greatly bless many other people for His glory.

Diligence in mapping out your financial future month-to-month and year-to-year and writing it down on paper is what it takes to repair damaged finances and maintain good financial health. A negative financial condition should make you turn from the money management principles you've been using and turn to bible principles, which always have your best interest in mind and result in blessings for you and other people.

If your situation is going to positively change, you must develop a monthly budget that lists all your bills and subtracts them from your net monthly income. Such budgeting shows, after all other bills are paid, what you have left to spend on personal items, savings, and investments. It should be calculated for each month for an extended period of times like six to twelve months.

This short-term planning of anticipated income and expenses is vital for bettering your financial health, because it lets you know what you can afford to purchase now and in the future. It shows how much money must remain in your account to cover deficits that will arise during future months and it shows how much money remains each month.

The remaining money should be used to give abundantly to the spread of the gospel, build at least a six-month emergency fund, and accumulate a size-able investment nest egg. It helps you care properly for yourself, your family, support godly ministry, and build wealth to serve your children.

You must keep the amount of expenses below your income in order to have peace in your life because this helps you take care of all your needs and responsibilities in life including you, your spouse, and children. You don't have to log all your expenses over the past few months nor log every single expense on a ledger for the next few months in order to decide what route to take to correct your situation. The pain of your present suffering should make you willing to follow biblical money management principles that help you establish a godly mission for your life, set proper goals, know your income, identify unnecessary expenses, and establish a budget for your family.

Many people don't like to hear the word "budget." However, when you don't develop a spending plan based on the reality of your present income then your reality throughout life will be that your expenses inevitably outgrow your income and leave you in financial turmoil with many headaches, torment, and bill collectors hounding you and credit card companies raising your interest rate to take even more from you while you suffer financially.

By counting the cost first - identifying your income and spending priorities on paper or computer via a budget – you turn your dream of financial freedom into a reality because it helps you spend less than you receive in a pay period so you can get out of debt in the most expedient manner. It helps identify your needs versus your wants, so you can focus on purchasing materials and services that have the highest priority.

Some advisors say people should budget by saving as much as they can afford and then be free to spend all the rest of the money at their disposal, but I say unto you create a giving, saving, spending plan. They say start with 2 to 3% of your pay, if you can, and later save more when you can afford to, but I say unto you do everything you can to increase your income and right-size your spending to enable you to tithe to the LORD's Church and save at least 10% of your gross income. They say a budget recognizes that taking out some types of loans to get what you want when you want it is acceptable, but the best situation *(which you can achieve)* is to owe no one anything but love and refuse to be a slave to lenders, because for the majority of people debt reduces the ability to properly care for things important to *(1)* the LORD, *(2)* their families, *(3)* wealth-building.

The problem with these advisors' point-of-view is *(a)* the priority they put on doing all you can to first get all the temporal material things you want, *(b)* it motivates you to put off saving when you do not feel like you can do it, and *(c)* it has no spiritual focus that pleases the LORD such as giving to spread the gospel, make disciples, and help others that are truly in need. This is not the proper priority of heart and mind for you. You should think and act upon GIVING first, SAVING next, and then upon SPENDING to care for responsibilities. Fulfilling the bulk of your desires through spending should come well after you are adhering to the first two principles.

The improper spending-based view of managing money makes it easy to condone taking on debt to keep up the lifestyle you want instead of shedding debt in order to be in good financial condition. In the spending-based form of budgeting *(which some people try to masquerade as saving-based budgeting)* the debt monster will eat you up and bring turmoil into your life. Because the focus is much too much on the spending side of the equation, you will set aside only a little savings and later must deplete those savings to pay on debts you should not have incurred in the first place. Finally, not knowing what to do, you will inevitably stop saving altogether and continue to take on more debt to do your own thing until you are stressed out and pressed out with monthly debt payments, high finance charges, and credit scores spiraling down as your ability to pay all the debts decreases.

Satan always attacks by tempting us to fulfill the lust of the flesh and eyes and to operate in the pride of life. He wants us to have our priorities in the wrong order and to keep them there. He knows that when he can keep you focused upon your material desires your ability to serve and be an example of Christ-likeness will remain hidden from view and may be entirely non-existent.

How you manage money that comes into your life is a very telling barometer of your spiritual condition because if you love Jesus Christ you will keep His commandments. No one can make money and the LORD their top priority at the same time. The bible provides specific instructions as to how true faith motivates us to do good works through the acquiring of income and the giving, saving, and spending of it.

Budgeting does not have to be complicated. If you will remember the priority that is in His heart and faithfully use it as you write down on paper / computer how you will manage the income He entrusts to you, then you will do well in the budgeting arena and thus bring more blessing into your life.

GIVING to the work of Christ via tithing and a free-will offering should be accounted for first in your budget and given to your local Church and worthwhile gospel teaching / preaching / good works ministries.

Next, you should SAVE a reasonable portion of your income. First as a $1,000 emergency fund to help cover rainy days. After all consumer debt is eliminated you should grow it to $10,000. Then focus on creating a wealth building foundation by investing at least 10% of your gross income in a diversified array of at least seven different no load low expense stock index mutual funds that over the past several decades have historically produced returns equivalent to the average annual growth of the American stock market over the past hundred years *(approximately 11%)*. Remember, you will get older, desire to live comfortably, travel, care for yourself when inevitable rainy days and health issues arise, and give abundantly to gospel work throughout your life.

Finally, you should focus on making sure you SPEND without taking on debt. Spending should be primarily focused on taking care of the most important priorities such as reasonable housing, food, clothing, and transportation. Fulfilling desires can and will come once you have put yourself on good financial footing and find that you have much greater disposable income.

Right-sizing spending means right now you may be unable to purchase unnecessary material things. You can use your Giving, Saving, Spending plan *(income statement / cash flow plan)* and wealth building statements *(net worth / balance sheet)* to help you determine when to purchase specific desirable things in a manner that will not put your finances in jeopardy or derail the LORD's plan for you to enter the Wealthy Place. Getting in His financial flow will please

Him and allow you to afford some of these things in the future while you are also able to avoid irresponsible money management behavior that leads to foreclosure, bankruptcy, and the inability to properly care for your family and personal responsibilities.

Faith in Him and His way of managing finances also causes Him to move in the hearts of other people *(at times when it would truly be a blessing to you)* to give you desired goods without you having to purchase them or engage debt bondage to get them.

Satan uses finances as an avenue of negative influence by convincing Christians that the LORD has no money management standards and instructions, nor rewards for those who adhere to them. In such Christians, giving to spread the gospel is almost null and void when measured against the income they receive. Not only are they not spreading the gospel with their mouths, they are also not involved in spreading the gospel by giving to a local Church and missionary endeavors. Satan has waged an all-out war and we must recognize it in order to have spiritual and economic victory over the enemy!

The heart of those that give sparingly lead them to actions that keep their resources from being greatly used by Him to bless others and lead them into a relationship with Jesus Christ and from being used to discipline themselves so they can be released from financial bondage.

They speak of proportionate giving as a biblical instruction, but only so they can give a smaller proportion of their income to the LORD's work over the years *(and feel good about it)* in order to fund the materialism inherent in their selfish thoughts & lifestyles. They sometimes mock other Christians who believe in giving at a higher level *(tithing, etc.)*. They believe some people are too poor to give to help spread the gospel. Some argue with other Christians accusing them of preaching or operating in legalism. However, Abraham and Jacob tithed before the law was ever written and scripture points to the action being directed by faith and it continues to lead many people out of financial bondage and into a spiritually disciplined lifestyle that gives them greater opportunity to fund the gospel message and lead people to Jesus Christ. The naysayers often expend minimal effort spreading the gospel and leading people to Jesus Christ, yet spend a lot of time disputing Christians over issues on which they do not really understand.

Learn to be grateful for other people's abundant giving even though you may not be at that place right now. Continue to ask the LORD to show you His will via study of the whole counsel in the bible. He will lead you to be a believer with a heart to give abundantly so you can be used by the LORD to a greater degree throughout your life to shine His light and pour His love on other people. He promises that those who sow abundantly will reap abundantly.

Knowing the state of your finances at all times is essential to obtain financial health, wealth, peace, and joy. Indeed, it is a part of pressing forward to the high calling of Christ, being like-minded with Him and His saints, and holding true to that which you have attained through salvation. In this way, you will maintain the maximum ability to have maximum fruitfulness He desires you to have in this earthly portion of your eternal life.

PRINCIPLE 8: Eliminate debt and move forward living debt-free.
Deuteronomy 28:12, 15, 44, Proverbs 22:6-7, Romans 13:8

The borrower is a slave to the lender. The LORD desires that you be the head and not the tail and this only happens financially when you eliminate debt and commit to living debt-free.

People and advertising constantly lead you to immediately pursue a lifestyle above what your income can currently provide. They entice you to spend everything you receive and to borrow even more money as the way to have it all. The problem is you have not been told about the grief that accompanies indebtedness and the financial situations that often result from it like inability to pay all your bills, repossession, foreclosure, and bankruptcy. On top of that creditors continue to contact you and press you to get the money you owe them. The stress of these situations often negatively affects your mental, emotional, physical, and spiritual health.

Those in debt generally feel like they work to support their creditors! They see creditors building great wealth for their businesses and personal lives. The purchase of material things over the years does not lead to the indebted person's wealth accumulation because the value of those items depreciates rapidly after the purchase to a level far below the purchase price. Many of these items have absolutely no value just a few months or years after purchase.

Debt is insidious because the seemingly small monthly payments lead people to get even more debt, which eventually accumulates to monthly payments and other bills close to or higher than their take home pay. Then, they experience a cash flow shortage in their personal and/or business finances. While it leads them down this path, their credit history gets much worse and they are charged higher interest rates which give creditors more of their money on top of principal payments. We have been consciously and subconsciously bombarded with messages and trained to follow this pathway such that we have now incorporated it into most every area of our life, such as buying cars, recreational vehicles, furniture, jewelry, clothing, mortgages, education *(school loans)*, etc.

Lenders and worldly financial counselors never tell you "The rich rules over the poor, and the borrower *is* servant to the lender" *(Proverbs 22:7 NKJV)* or "There is desirable treasure, and oil in the dwelling of the wise, but a foolish man squanders it." *(Proverbs 21:20 NKJV)*. If you want misery throughout your life, continue to follow the ways of the world by continuing to borrow more and more and refusing to pursue debt freedom. However, you do have another option. You can put on the mind of Christ to engage good money management. By doing so, you heap to yourself the financial benefits you otherwise pay to those you borrow money from.

This process starts by *(a)* refusing to borrow any more money, *(b)* seeking additional income you can use to totally eliminate debt over the next year or two, *(c)* budgeting responsibly, *(d)* foregoing purchase of all unneeded material things until you are debt-free, and *(e)* trusting Him to provide needs when you don't have cash to purchase them. Your debt will be eliminated shortly and over time you'll accumulate massive savings and investments and a heart to give abundantly to endeavors that glorify the LORD. For the rest of your life, instead of creditors making lots of money off you, you will make lots of money off the interest and growth you get from your savings and equity investments.

This strategy seeks to minimize the amount of finance charges you pay during the process of eliminating debt. Before using this approach it's best to close all retail store charge cards and cut them up, so you won't be tempted to use them again because they charge you nearly twenty-five cents on the dollar in interest. At most, keep a low-interest visa type account for extreme emergencies, if you can truly be responsible by not charging anything more unless an extreme emergency occurs for which you simply have no cash to cover. However, after a year or so of disciplined debt repayment and saving in an emergency fund you should not be in this type of situation.

You should consolidate as much higher interest debt as possible onto this card so you can more quickly pay off your debts if the visa type card allows you to transfer other card balances and pay interest on them at rates lower than what you are currently paying on the retail store charge cards. If you're prone to undisciplined spending and charging purchases you should apply for a low-interest closed-ended consolidation loan instead so whatever amount is paid off is not re-chargeable.

If you have equity in your house you may be able to consolidate credit card and other debt into a mortgage or home equity loan. Such loans usually charge much lower interest rates than would be charged by credit card companies. The interest you pay on these loans can generally be deducted on your federal tax returns to reduce the amount of taxes you would otherwise owe. If you decide to use these methods to help pay down your debt beware that the financial institution can start foreclosure proceedings on your home if you miss a payment. This could result in the loss of your home and equity that you've built up over many years. That is why it is not good in many instances to use home loans to pay off other consumer debt.

Each of these methods requires you to become and remain disciplined in spending and saving in order for them to work to benefit you. They are not for the faint of heart, rather they are for those who are resolute and disciplined in their desire to be a godly steward of their money, eliminate their debt, and become debt-free. Such people are willing to make necessary sacrifices to help themselves reach this financial position. They will engage biblical financial principles such as tracking income and expenses, cutting spending, reading financial literature to learn more about how to properly manage, honoring Him by giving to help spread the gospel and help others, and saving for rainy days and future purposes.

This process starts by saying no to any loan for items that depreciate in value when you cannot immediately pay cash for them and when accepting the credit won't immediately benefit you by allowing your savings to accumulate at a higher interest rate than the interest rate you would pay the creditor on the loan balance.

It's impossible to meet these requirements with most types of borrowing, including revolving credit card and store charge card accounts, because most institutions that offer such credit charge you very high interest rates. For example, the interest rate for most store charge cards is usually greater than 20%. While the interest rate for some credit cards can be lower, by accepting them you're generally allowing the credit card issuer to raise interest rates sometime down the road if it believes you then represent greater risk of not paying or not paying on time, etc.

For the most part the rates on these cards hover in the teens and are much too high to presume that you can invest and generate more growth than you'll pay out in interest to your creditors. This inability to generate greater growth does not even encompass the various penalties you will pay if you are not able to meet the card issuer's payment requirements down the road.

There is a very small percentage of people who have played the leverage game and seem to have beaten the system. Historically, there has always been a small group of people who financed their business ventures using credit cards or other loans and then experienced a surge in customer purchases producing revenue that seems to overcome interest they pay on the loans. This small group that represents less than one percent of business owners who have tried this method. Don't let their supposed success fool you into thinking this is a prudent strategy for financing your business. Most who try this method go in the red and belly up a short time thereafter.

Biblical instruction strongly guides you to pursue your financial life *(personal and business)* from a debt-free mindset; asking the LORD and seeking a number of godly counselors who can help you find prudent ways to start and invest in business endeavors and purchase personal merchandise desirable to you and within your budget. The vast majority of people I've met who did not follow this method have found themselves in financial turmoil at some point in their lives and the turmoil for many continues today because they still refuse to utilize biblical money management instruction to guide their financial affairs.

If you have a history of undisciplined use of credit cards, then you should immediately discipline yourself to stop using them, build at least three months of income in an emergency reserve account, and even eventually cut up the ones you have and throw them away because they will continue to bring torment into your life.

If you are a disciplined spender who stays well within established budget boundaries, a low interest revolving credit card will generally not hurt you because you will only use it for convenience and record-keeping purposes where you will only make purchases already accounted for in your budget and you never charge more on these cards than the amount of cash you have available in the bank minus your monthly bills, saving, investing, tithing, and giving.

Scripture strongly advises you to live debt-free because the LORD desires debt-freedom for you. The compounding interest nature of most debt will wreck your ability to build wealth for the future. The enemy knows this and tempts you to satisfy the cravings of your flesh using debt instruments. However, when you commit to His plan of living debt-free He will provide your every need without you having to borrow to supply it. When you refuse to take on debt, you enable the LORD to supernaturally provide by moving others to provide needs and desires at no cost when you're unable to purchase them.

He desires that you be debt-free. He wants this for your personal life and business ownership. Many have ignored His instructions and warnings about debt and others have compromised His standards not believing that it is possible to be debt-free. While a few people wind up appearing better off because they leveraged consumer debt, the vast majority of people are destroying peace and joy in their lives by taking on excessive debt.

A legitimate reason for taking on debt is when parents have no way to provide food and/or shelter during a period of poverty in which severe hardship has overtaken the family. It may also be acceptable to use debt instruments whenever you have fixed assets of an amount that covers the total loan plus interests and costs and enough stable income or cash flow to cover the monthly payments. This scenario describes many real estate purchases for a family's primary home, rental property, flipping, or commercial property.

The latter type of indebtedness *(real estate mortgage)* is considered shrewd by some people because the asset may increase in value to be far greater than the outstanding amount of the loan and because renting the property may create enough cash flow *(income)* to more than cover the monthly loan payment and any other expenses resulting from ownership of the assets. In such situations, you earn more on your money than you pay out in interest on the loan. Some call it using the world's money to make a fortune for the kingdom.

Yet, you must be very careful when walking this path because many people with good intentions were not able to produce enough cash flow to cover the loan payments and/or the value of the asset dropped due to market conditions. In many of these situations, people *(Christians also)* were forced to file bankruptcy or had the properties foreclosed on and wound up with huge amounts of debt still being pursued by bill collectors and in some cases the government.

When people compromise by taking on debt instruments without the net worth to cover the entire amount of indebtedness, they usually shortchange the kingdom of God and the Church and bring financial hardship upon their families. Unfortunately, one bad choice is never enough for them, so they enter into such situations with many creditors for mortgages, car notes, visas, charge cards, etc. This eliminates disposable income that could be used to invest and grow wealth and puts them in a position where they choose to pay creditors instead of paying tithes to their local Church to help lead people to Jesus Christ and teach them how to walk in His ways.

While most people want blessings and rewards from the LORD, they unfortunately give worldly methods more allegiance. Your vision should be focused on the fact that He is able to prosper you and grow great wealth for your family without you getting into debt. He wants to bring you out of debt, not further encumber your life with debt. Debt freedom is truly the best position to work yourself into. It's wonderful to know His vision for you is that large and He is powerful enough to help you make it happen!

Satan has given the principality mammon an assignment to lead our nation and its individual citizens into massive spending of borrowed money. He has been working over many decades to turn people's hearts away from doing all they can to fund and carry out the Great Commission. He encourages them to seek pleasure at all costs. He motivates them to make their will their chief aim. And, he gives the illusion that "the person with the most toys or money is happiest and wins the game."

This could not be farther from the truth. The bible declares that dwelling in the LORD's Kingdom provides the only righteousness, peace, and joy. This state of eternity, heart, and mind comes only when you are faithful with what He has given you and trust Him enough to honor Him first by giving back to gospel ministry in proportion to all that He entrusts to you. When you regard His will above your own pleasures, He is just as happy with you as He is with the widow that gave two mites into the temple treasury, regardless of whether you are rich or poor.

About two percent of the people make millions and can afford to have lots of things without borrowing to make it happen. Most of the other ninety-eight percent try to live in that same mode but must borrow heavily in order to give the appearance they've reached the pinnacle of success or to have the kinds of pleasures they have been convinced they should have.

Let's be clear, these days there are many who have made millions and lost it because they too tried to leverage their way into much more by unreasonably using debt instruments. I could name numerous businessmen, entertainers, actors, and professional athletes that have thrown themselves into this category by ungodly stewardship of money. No doubt, many people that never made it to that level of wealth do the same thing every day. So, this is not a rich man's problem or a poor man's problem. It is a bondage to satan problem.

Many people get into financial trouble and then try to get out of the trouble the same way they got into it: by borrowing more money hoping something about their situation will change to allow them to pay what they owe their lenders. I have seen such unwise stewardship lead to greater hardships for many people not very far down the road. Other people filed for bankruptcy in order to eliminate as much debt as possible, but shortly afterward went right back to borrowing to please their flesh by getting more stuff. In the process, they paid much higher finance charges on material purchases; as high as 30%

on cars and 20% on mortgages. What they thought was a smart financial move was actually in conflict with scripture and within a short time they suffered greater financial hardship than before.

He desires that His people and Church be debt-free. If you want to see your financial position change you must change your money management habits by honoring Him with the first fruits of your income, getting yourself in position to save and invest, and curtailing your spending and borrowing through the use of budgeting. Don't fall into satan's trap. Draw close to Him and learn His will for your well-being and pursue it. Then, you can be sure He will provide all your need according to His riches in glory in Christ Jesus *(Philippians 4:19)* as you take action to owe no person anything but love.

A lifestyle that moves you to eliminating all debt, including mortgages, always betters your long-term financial condition because it positions you to always be able to honor Him with your tithes and offerings so Heaven's windows are open to pour out greater income on you.

Some financial advisors tell people it is not good to pay off a current mortgage because you can make more money by investing in the stock market or by leveraging your money to obtain more loans to get investment real estate and the monthly rental payments they believe will come from it. However, this is tricky at best because even with investment advice most people are not good enough investors to be able to get greater annual investment return than the interest charged on their mortgage*(s)*.

Financial advisors have their place and reputable ones should be consulted to help educate you to be a responsible manager of the money entrusted to you and to help you maintain emotional composure and reasonable investment allocation / diversification when the economic environment looks good, bad, or indifferent over short and long periods of time. But you should not use them because you believe they have the ability to pick the greatest investments and guarantee gains on investments. For good reason the SEC requires investment firms to put the following type of statement on their investment literature, "Past investment returns are no guarantee of future investment results."

In addition, most people are simply not good landlords and managers of rental property or good at fixing up and flipping properties. So, they lose money on these investment choices and find that over the years they are not in a better financial position than if they had simply paid off their mortgage and saved and reasonably invested over the course of the years of their lives. The problem is exacerbated when the properties are not within close proximity to where they live.

Another thing that people are often told by financial advisors, accountants, and tax preparers is that they should keep their mortgages because of the tax reduction that the interest payments afford them each year. However, they usually make a flawed analysis of this situation in that the amount of interest you pay needs to be greater than the standard deduction on your federal tax return in order for you to itemize deductions to be able to get a tax reduction.

For this and other reasons, many people with mortgages do not itemize their federal tax returns. In addition, even if you could get a tax reduction, you should consider whether it is smart to pay $1,000 when you do not need to in order to get 15 to 25% of it returned via a tax reduction *($150 to $250)*, especially when you cannot get a guaranteed growth on the investment that you would supposedly engage. Let's be honest, most people will never make or maintain large investments when they don't employ rapid mortgage debt reduction plans. They usually spend the extra money on frivolous stuff they cannot remember a few years down the road. Yet, rapidly paying off your mortgage will build the right kind of discipline that is always remembered, cherished, and continued.

I understand part of the benefit you may get from a mortgage is the ability to get a house you want right now with the price locked in because you do not currently have the assets to immediately pay the full asking price. However, that does not make it smart to continue paying mortgage interest when you could in fact pay off the mortgage.

You will lift a great debt burden off your shoulders and will feel extreme freedom and will have removed the possibility that you could one day be in a situation where a financial institution is foreclosing on the home*(s)* that you have made monthly payments on for so long. You can at the point of mortgage payoff begin saving what was your monthly mortgage payment and then not have to worry about whether or not you can actually earn more than the mortgage interest amount.

You are also free to take extra investment risk with a portion of the money if you choose to do so without running into the possibility that you may one day owe financial institutions money you cannot pay them. This type of financial freedom relieves stress and pressure and puts you in a position where the LORD can entrust you with far more money and resources because you have proven to be a good steward whose eyes and actions are on Him and His way rather than the way of the world.

If debt elimination is best for mortgages, it is even better for other types of loans *(car notes, revolving charge cards, student loans, etc.)* because they generally offer none of the tax reduction options that home mortgages provide and have much higher finance charges.

That is why I implore you to save at least $1,000 dollar emergency fund, then pay off all non-home mortgage debt *(car loans, credit cards, etc.)*, then save at least $10,000, and more if you are self-employed or have uneven / uncertain monthly income. Then, pay off your mortgage as fast as you can by making extra, large principle payments on it.

Eliminating debt and being debt-free for ten, twenty, or more years will usually afford you with hundreds of thousands and sometimes millions of dollars more of assets from which you earn great growth and use of in order to properly care for your family, fund the gospel, pursue your God-given purpose, and enjoy good things without being stressed out and pressed out. Therefore, paying off loans always makes sense, so you are not ensnared by the awful consequences of debt that can so quickly overtake you when you least expect it.

PRINCIPLE 9: Refuse to cosign or become surety for anyone's debts.
Proverbs 6:1-2, Proverbs 11:15, Proverbs 17:18

Do not cosign for other people's debts unless you want your coat taken and want to be subject to ridicule and irresponsibility.

Cosigning *(surety)* on a debt is verbally committing or signing a contract that says you will pay the amount of money another person borrows when he does not meet the obligation to make the contractually required payments. Another form of cosigning is using your credit accounts *(Visa, Mastercard, etc.)* to make purchases for someone because you think they will pay you back. Almost every time you cosign, you will lose money because the person will not pay the loan as agreed and the creditor will come after you for payment.

Most people who could not pay cash for what they wanted or who did not have the good credit history necessary to borrow money on their own to make a purchase have not had the responsible nature necessary to show they are a good credit risk. Financial institutions have better systems to measure risk of default than you do. When they will not loan the person money without a cosigner then you should take heed and refuse to cosign.

Most people asking you to cosign will continue to be financially irresponsible and impatient in pursuing desires and in other financial dealings. In the end, this means that they will stop making agreed upon payments or fail to pay you back and then you will be required to make payments at some point, risk ruining your credit history, and put you in a bad financial situation.

Cosigning encourages people *(family, friends, etc.)* to remain financially irresponsible and untrustworthy. Refusing to cosign doesn't mean that along your path of life you should not help people. Feed a man you meet who is hungry, give clothes to a person that has none, and help find shelter for one that is homeless. There are many resources already in your cupboards, closets, and community you can use for this purpose.

If the person cannot afford to purchase a material thing he desires *(product or service he does not truly need)*, then he should not have it at this time. He should learn *(and when necessary you should teach him)* to work to meet his own desires on the income he receives and to trust the LORD to provide the means to meet needs without causing anyone to take on debt. When making purchases, you should be an example for him of a person who only uses available money above expenses necessary to meet your needs. When you do not have cash, he will see that you do not attempt to take out loans or get others to be surety to get it.

When you don't already have money in savings or investments to pay the full amount that would be borrowed, then you are not in a position to help the person to that degree. Even when you do have enough money to cover the full amount of the person's debt, you should still measure the situation to ensure you are not casting your pearls to swine. Do not waste resources the LORD entrusts to you on people who willfully disregard His instructions on good stewardship. Until they decide to follow His will and way and no matter what you do for them, they will continuously and irresponsibly spend and make bad financial decisions that continue to keep them in the position where they cannot purchase things they truly need and desire.

Watch, pray, and observe people to find out how you should help or instruct people who solicit use of your credit accounts and/or signature on loan contracts that benefit them. The devil is constantly searching for a way to encourage you to mismanage money so it is of no great use in helping fulfill the Great Commission via *(a)* prudently providing for your family, *(b)* giving to maintain and enhance your local Church outreach and discipleship ministry, and *(c)* giving to fund missions work through other people who are in places you cannot physically reach. Through failure to study and understand the bible, many people don't realize they're being used by the devil in this way. So, don't condemn them, just don't give in to the enemy's plan concerning money the LORD entrusts to you.

The best way to help others and ensure you are not an infidel *(irresponsible and untrustworthy)* who doesn't appropriately provide for your family and take care of your responsibilities is to use available cash or resources when a true need exists. Immediately discontinue cosigning and pray that those who approach you to cosign will allow the Holy Spirit to guide them in using biblical money management principles, so they can meet their God-given responsibilities.

Unfortunately, people cosign on debt for others by using their credit card*(s)* or by signing a note that says they will pay the loan amount if he / she is unable to. It didn't seem to matter to you that they wanted the material thing for a desire and not a need. Also, they never considered that He warns us not to cosign *(become surety)* for other people's debts. Further, it didn't appear to matter that they did not save a reasonable amount of money along the way for emergencies and situations they know will occur from time to time.

Continuing to have these types of response to a person's request for you to cover their debt will continue to place you in tight financial situations and will cause you to be irresponsible in taking care of your family and His business. Your money will soon be gone, no matter how much you have or make. You must watch and pray and observe those that labor among you. Remember, everyone sins and falls short of His best. In so doing, we have created bad habits in many areas of our lives, finances included. We need to be directed to walk the right pathway for handling our lives and finances so mistakes are not repeated and we do not live in continual financial bondage and beneath the privilege the LORD prepared for us.

The best way to help most people and yourself financially is to give them available cash if a true need arises. Definitely, discontinue cosigning and do not loan money to irresponsible people. Now, pray for and encourage them to use biblical principles to manage money and desires, so their true needs can be met. This includes practices like *(a)* tithing and free-will offering, *(b)* planning including budgeting income and expenses, *(c)* building/maintaining a reasonable emergency fund, *(d)* paying off all loans in order to live debt-free, *(e)* refusing to cosign, *(f)* saving and investing, *(g)* and diversifying investments. In this way, you will not help push them and yourself into greater financial bondage and the pain it produces. Instead you will be leading them down the path of abundant life the LORD prepared for each one of us.

Once you have refused a person's request to cosign, you must encourage him to use biblical money management principles. You should responsibly help those truly in need according to your ability. However, you must discern the devil's strategy to have you waste money on people who mismanage theirs and who do not regard bible instruction. He would have you squander money on funding their desires *(cars, houses, boats, etc.)* when it could be better spent leading people to Christ.

When a true need exists, it's best to give a person cash or resources you have on hand that you do not need to take care of your priority items like family, mortgage, rent, and bills you owe. People often think cosigning a loan will help others, however it inevitably enables the person to continue irresponsible behavior toward family and good stewardship. It moves them further away from practices that help properly care for family, Church, and other God-given responsibilities. You enable the person to forsake good stewardship habits that come only from the knowledge of His will, trials, errors, sacrifice, contentment, delayed gratification, and complete trust in Him.

Unless you see someone beaten up on the road who needs assistance right now or someone who is hungry and needs food, or who has some other emergency need problem that the person did not bring upon him or herself and will not continue to perpetuate by his or her continued mindset and activities, then you should really, really know the person to know whether or not he or she is truly in need but is normally responsible or is really ready to become responsible. This helps you be prudent in providing the type of help that will truly help him or her take care of the abnormal situation or get out of the irresponsible activities that led to the situation.

Of course, there are times where you extend help to people in the community or in another part of the world, simply because you've identified an emergency need. Sometimes, we don't know the entire background of the situation at hand and whether or not the person is irresponsible and it led to the sad situation. So, whenever the Holy Spirit directs you to help a person or give to a need, you should obey Him in order for the best to come to pass, for Him to bring what is important to the attention of the person being helped, and for it to be an example to others of completely trusting the LORD's guidance.

He never asks you to do anything in a way that violates scriptural commands or principles found in the bible. This should be a basis for how you measure the person's situation and for determining the help you can give or sometimes the help you should not give. The bible never encourages people to take on monetary debt through borrowing or cosigning. So, don't cosign for anyone unless you already have the money saved in a safe and sound place and are truly prepared to pay off the entire loan when they default on it.

When you have cosigned a note for someone, the bible tells you to quickly go to the lender and attempt to remove your name off the debt. In many instances the person you cosigned for will fail to pay the loan as required and the creditor will go after your collateral or income to pay the bill. Please don't fall out with a friend because you failed to make the right decision by refusing to cosign for his debt. After all, your failure is one of the reasons he / she continues to be irresponsible in financial dealings. Continue to love, pray for financial wisdom, stay away from co-signing, and trust and obey biblical financial principles as an example to him / her. This takes the pressure and stress off you trying to be your friend's financial savior and helps show Jesus Christ should be the author and finisher of his / her faith who will lead them to a better spiritual and financial condition.

When you're approached by family and friends about co-signing, tell them "NO" and continue to pray for strength to be wise according to His word and that they will see and act upon biblical money management principles in the future so they can receive the great benefits produced by following them.

Many times, people that ask you to co-sign could take initiative to resolve their situation without asking you to take on their debt. However, they don't see the picture clearly or they simply want to use a way that appears easier for them. For example, the person could get up earlier to catch the bus to work instead of asking you to co-sign for a car note. Or, the person could purchase a less expensive engagement ring for their fiancé instead of asking you to co-sign for a more expensive ring. Or, the person could rent, pay off debts, and begin to save for a 20% down payment on a home instead of asking you to co-sign on a home loan.

This lesson is not to discourage from giving to meet true needs. Christians should be givers and lend themselves to abundantly funding gospel ministry and helping the poor. Pursuant to biblical instruction, I am instructing you to stay away from promising to cover debts taken by other people when you don't currently have far more than enough money to cover the entire debt because history shows most of them (at some point not too long after you cosign) will ultimately refuse or be unable to complete their promise and commitment to paying the debt. Co-signing will set you up for a financial fall that you could have and should have avoided.

Stop cosigning for family and friends to get things they can't afford to pay cash for. The best way to help most people and ensure your long-term financial health is to give them available cash when a true and verified need arises in their lives. Then encourage them to use biblical principles to manage their money and desires, so their needs can be met.

PRINCIPLE 10: Save and Invest.
Proverbs 13:23, Proverbs 21:20, Matthew 25:14-30, Luke 19:12-27

Save and invest a reasonable portion of your income to produce greater profit. There is oil and wine in the dwelling of the wise but a foolish man spends all he gets his hands on. The LORD commended the faithful servants who traded with what He gave them and produced double to present to Him.

When you spend all your income and continually obtain loans and use credit cards to get everything you want, the day will come when you will have a mountain of bills you cannot pay. Some worldly pundits tout paying yourself first as the solution to all your financial problems. However, that method does not work, unless you always remember your monthly net after-tax income and consistently spend less than that amount minus what you pay yourself first during the month. Otherwise, you will eventually stop paying yourself first and borrow it all back via credit cards and other loans in order to obtain needed cash to pay creditors that have cajoled you into an unreasonable lifestyle given the income you thus far earn.

Do not be fooled, whether you are considered rich or poor, you can get into a habit of spending more than your net income. The bible instructs you to write your vision down on paper, so you can remember it and take steps to achieve it using His supernatural guidance & power. It contains a pattern where believers accumulated wealth from legitimate work and inheritances that would be used to carry out His will and take care of their families at the current time and into the future. Consider the faith of Abraham and Sarah, Jacob, Boaz and Ruth, King David, Mordecai and Esther, Joseph of Arimathea, Barnabas, and Lydia.

Undoubtedly, some of the patriarchs and matriarchs suffered trials, tribulations, and even poverty at certain points in their lives. We also know that some of them committed sin on occasion. Yet, the Father was faithful to restore them when they repented and continued to build trust in Him. The bible gives no indication whatsoever that the accumulation of wealth they experienced was sinful or in conflict with His will and in fact it acknowledges their wealth as a blessing from the LORD as they used it for righteous endeavors.

The instruction of scripture is to make sure our devotion to Jesus Christ is our number one priority. Seek His face *(intimacy)* and not His hand *(material things)*. When you seek His face, all you need and more is provided to fulfill His plan for your life and it happens without you exhibiting greedy, covetous, and selfish traits.

The accumulation of wealth from godliness is the result of the LORD opening Heaven's windows and pouring out a blessing you cannot contain and you managing *(giving, saving, and spending it)* in accordance with biblical principles for good stewardship. It is clear in scripture you should seek to save and invest a portion of the manifold blessings He provides you.

The bible doesn't identify a specific amount you should save and invest, yet wisdom should lead you to set aside at least ten percent of your gross pay, since it is similar to the tithe the bible exhorts Christians to provide the Church for the spread of the gospel.

Scripture tells us Christians should be led by the Holy Spirit who lives in them because He will lead us to Jesus Christ, His will, and His way of being and doing things as it comports with the scripture. In other words, in Christ your life will have the balance required to accomplish everything you are called to accomplish on Earth and to store as treasure in Heaven.

Christ's balance for you will look unbalanced to some people and they may express negative comments about His way of doing things. However, when you are not balanced according to His calling, your life is ripe for destruction initiated by satan and brought about by ungodly morals and the actions produced by them. People who get off His narrow path usually fall into one of two financial extremes:

- Stinginess, which is displayed by failing to faithfully support gospel work in the Earth via tithes and offerings through their local Church and other worthwhile ministries.
- Materialism, which is displayed by purchasing an abundance of material things while refusing to prepare for a rainy season in proportion to the income the LORD entrusted to them.

People in these extremes wrongly think money and/or things provide the protection, security, and favor they need. They also think they will miss something in life if they don't spend all their income and credit getting material things to appease their flesh and impress others. These mindsets are unproductive for your future and allow problems to overtake you at some point in your life, not far down the road. In addition, such mindsets fail to display the kind of trust you need to have in the LORD's grace to help you be and do everything you are called to do.

Only the LORD provides truly valuable eternal and earthly blessings. Failing to use godly stewardship to manage the money entrusted to you, which includes saving and investing, will put you in an uncomfortable position because catastrophic and emergency situations will arise throughout your life. These situations will require money and resources to alleviate.

Don't succumb to the two extremes that result from falling off of His path for you. Instead, allow Him to instill the proper balance for life and money management. From this pathway, you will do things that will help you proceed and succeed throughout your life such as faithfully tithing, offering, caring for your family, and filling your life with fellowship and ministry to Him and people.

You can start this process by reducing your spending on needless material purchases, so you can save as much as possible and build an appropriate emergency fund. After you've reached that goal and paid off all non-mortgage debt, put additional disposable income into savings and investments *(reputable stock and bond mutual funds and fixed-income accounts)* that provide diversity and won't put the funds in unreasonable financial jeopardy.

I hope hard times never come upon you and pray the LORD sustains the Church in good and bad economic times, yet Proverbs 23:20 shows wise people save a reasonable portion of income whereas foolish people spend all they get and Ecclesiasts 11:2 exhorts you to invest a portion of your income with seven or eight sources because you do not know when bad economic times will encroach on your home and family.

Just remember, savings and investments are not your source. They're only a resource the LORD allows you to set aside to provide help in time of need: maybe for yourself, maybe for others, probably for both. Never be worried about the amount of your accumulation. Simply work hard and be a good steward according to biblical instruction concerning giving, saving, and spending and you will find that the amounts that you accumulate over time will be immensely helpful in carrying out His will for your life.

Many people get laid off, receive less pay, and have their overall assets reduced during times of stock market correction, recession, and depression. One has only to review the history of the U.S. and world economies to recognize that these times will come. Yet, by failing to save, invest, and live in accordance with biblical principles many people act as if they're oblivious to the fact that these economic situations will arise at some point.

Unfortunately, most people engage in personal money management practices that will land them in financial turmoil at some point in their lives, especially when several of the major markets are down, such as stock and real estate. Turmoil occurs because they continue to do things the world's way like taking on ever increasing debt to purchase material things beyond the reach of their current income and assets. Many also fail to honor the LORD in tithing for the spread of the gospel and work of the ministry. At the same time, others spend all their resources on get- rich-quick business ventures and supposed high-earning investment schemes marketed by people whose promises turn out to be untrustworthy.

They fail to realize that you cannot listen to anyone who tells you a specific investment method or type of business is successful for everyone who uses it *(without historical data proving it)*. You should refuse to listen to the scam artists and only listen and obey biblical instruction which shows all believers should follow specific financial principles such as diligently performing a God-pleasing type of work, tithing, offering, planning finances *(including budgeting)*, spending far less than 89% of your gross pay, saving, investing, eliminating all debt, and refusing to take on future debt, and diversifying assets.

The heavy concentration you put in one investment or industry will usually turn into a financial downfall for you, especially when you do not gain expertise in how that market operates in hopes of avoiding downturns or accumulating enough income and assets to weather storms. When you engage in such risky get-rich-quick endeavors you will suffer foreclosure, bankruptcy, unrecoverable losses, and/or great discomfort for a lengthy time in order to get back to the place where He wanted you to be all along.

He has done preventative maintenance by putting investment principles in the bible that help us overcome the severe effects of economic downturn. This doesn't mean that you'll never be touched by storms or that you should take no business or investment risks. Every person will face obstacles and catastrophes in life and every investment carries the risk that it may not grow and that the investor might lose principal. However, you always have a better chance of maintaining your lifestyle, giving, saving, investing, and recovering losses when you consistently make two actions part of your financial plan:

1. Diligently work to get out and stay out of debt by regularly paying down and ultimately paying off everything from credit card debt to car loans to home mortgages.
2. Diversify assets by buying seven or eight different types of investments.

These principles help you overcome the downturns that affect every investment market. Historically, down markets do not affect every industry or investment at the same time, so using these two principles allows you to be in a place where you're not negatively affected or moved by current economic winds. You can spend whatever income you receive to meet your needs without having bill collectors chasing you to pay debts you cannot afford. Also, you have a much greater possibility of annual asset growth when only a few markets are down at the same time because the growth of investments you have in markets that are up have an opportunity to outweigh the losses you will experience in markets that are down.

As you can see, He provided insulation against economic upheaval, but you must do your part to employ His plan so you are always in a position where you can come out ahead no matter what economic / financial obstacles come your way. Don't let satan deceive you into thinking that you cannot manage your current lifestyle and income to build wealth just because you are currently receiving government assistance, have minimum wage income, or a lot of bills. No matter what your income it will be managed one way or another: either poorly or successfully.

So, do yourself a favor and save yourself from anguish by committing to manage money successfully in a way that glorifies the LORD and helps bring His will to pass in your life and the lives of others He has called you to minister to. The only way to successfully manage money is to follow biblical instruction. Pray and ASK Him to show you in the bible what you should focus on with regard to giving, saving, and spending. Then, SEEK to do it by writing on paper or computer the long-term vision *(plan)* and short and mid-term steps *(budget)* you will engage. Then, KNOCK on the door by following the budget, so you can fulfill the vision to which you are called. Budget sheets, software, and instructions are available from many different online sources to help you employ this principle.

Each item on the budget is a goal that directs how you allocate your dollars to help you fulfill the vision. Written budgets glorify

Him because they plainly write vision so you can take necessary steps to fulfill purpose. Also, scripture instructs a man to count the cost prior to trying to build anything. In addition, Proverbs tells people to know the state of their assets, income, and expenses so that they are able to build wealth and so it can endure from generation to generation.

A wise man will save a portion of the income while a foolish man spends everything he gets. Also, a wise person tithes and gives knowing the LORD will provide everything needed for life and fulfillment of purpose. However, a foolish man fails to give because He does not trust Him to provide what is needed. A wise man spends in ways that glorify the LORD and not material things, recognizing He is the source and things given from His hand are not to be worshipped or adored. However, a foolish man spends without regard to His desire believing that having more, different, or opulent things will satisfy the soul with peace and joy.

Can you see how the foolish man's vision and goals are twisted and warped in a way that will not allow him to be successful, build wealth, and engage ministry in a way that pleases Him? Don't let your current income level or financial situation dictate your vision and actions, otherwise you'll continue to be in financial turmoil. That is not the legacy you want to live in or leave behind.

Saving is generally considered money put away in vehicles that preserve the principle amount. Usually, the money earns a lower percentage of interest on a regular periodic basis. Also, it can be accessed quickly when needed. Usually, it focuses on seen and unforeseen expenses that might occur in the short-term *(a period less than five years)* for things like roof repairs, furnace repairs, hospital emergencies, etc.

Investing is often thought of for the long-term horizon *(five years or more)*. It would normally be used for things like building retirement savings, funding a business or ministry dream that will take years to finally engage, saving for a child's college tuition, etc.

The person who invests should understand that he will not earn periodic interest and that the value of the investment at any given time *(whether increased or decreased from the time he bought it)* is subject to supply and demand for that investment. Also, he may lose principle and should be willing to take that risk hoping that he will instead experience greater growth in value during the many years he holds the investment.

Investing should usually be done after you have been disciplined to use good money management practices like consistently earning an income, adhering to a budget that keeps your monthly expenses below 70% of your take home pay, consistently giving money for ministry that leads people to Jesus Christ, saving an amount equal to six-months of take home pay as an emergency reserve account, eliminating all debts, and committing to never co-signing for anyone else's loans/debts.

Because most of us are not market experts and stock picking gurus, we should utilize a process called dollar cost averaging whereby we automatically buy on a periodic basis *(weekly or monthly)* a certain dollar amount of diversified investments with solid historical track records from a brokerage house like Vanguard or through our employer's deferred compensation plan *(401k, 457, 403b, etc.)*. This helps us exercise the buy low, sell high principle that leads to investment success and wealth building. Those who do otherwise are trying to time the market and are usually doing so without proper investment education. The vast majority suffer extreme losses over time and never wind up building the wealth they envisioned and hastily went after.

No matter the style, with investments past results are no guarantee of future returns. However, you should have greater comfort being invested after your financial stewardship is in order. Down the road *(after 5 or more years of holding good investments)*, they will put you in a much better financial position and help you overcome inflationary pressures that might otherwise diminish the purchasing power of money in savings accounts.

Here are a few helpful guidelines you can use when the time comes for you to add investing to your good stewardship repertoire:

- Review the prospectus for each investment to see its one-year, five-year, and ten-year investment returns. Make sure they meet or exceed benchmark returns for that type of investment.
- Identify its expense ratio. Stay away from any investment where it is not well under one percent of the assets under management.
- Make sure no more than 10% of your investment dollars are put into any one investment. Proper diversification and asset allocation are generally best for everyone.
- Start with no-load low-expense mutual funds until you are very knowledgeable about and skilled in capturing growth in the value of other types of investments *(individual stocks, real estate, futures, oil & gas leases, etc.)*.

Many of the mutual funds you choose to purchase will have an electronic funds transfer provision that will allow you to immediately start investing in them by giving the brokerage house authorization to electronically transfer as little as $50 per month out of your savings or checking account that it will use to purchase shares of the mutual fund*(s)* you want.

The electronic funds transfer option allows you to avoid the minimum start-up investment *(normally $1,000 or more)* that many funds require for people who send checks to the investment firm. If you can't or don't wish to use an electronic funds transfer option, then it's worth your while to save the amount of money needed to meet the required minimum investment for the investment vehicle you want to invest in.

Investing is a great wealth building tool that can enhance your life and ministry. It also helps you better capture increased monetary value that can be used to abundantly give in the future in a way that enhances the lives of many others. I know quite a number of people that have become very wealthy using simple biblical financial principles while at the same time tithing and giving abundant offerings for ministry work locally and abroad. The legacy you leave this earth that determines the treasure stored up for you in Heaven should be to learn and take action to be the best possible steward you can.

PRINCIPLE 11: Diversifying savings and investments.
Proverbs 15:22, Ecclesiastes 11:2, Matthew 25:14, Luke 19:12

There is safety in the multitude of counselors. Therefore, save and invest with seven or eight different reputable sources and with a similar number of different types of investments.

Working diligently to serve, gain experience, and develop skill that produce income to care for yourself and your family and help provide for others in need is certainly the road to take. It will help you have more provision for yourself, family, and other worthwhile priorities as opposed to the meager welfare that might be afforded by other people when you choose the other route of not seeking to consistently work.

Many forces in the world seek to pull you away from the above foundations of good stewardship by telling you that some other principle is more important in our modern, civilized society, such as having access to as much personal credit *(loans)* as you can get your hands on. Advisors are telling people they cannot live without credit and they should keep credit card accounts open at all cost. Other people are saying you will always have bills or car notes or house notes. Finance journalists, advisors, and pundits are saying you need to have all of these in order to keep your credit score as high as possible.

For the unsuspecting and those ignorant of truth this sounds like savvy advice. However, you should understand none of Jesus commandments and principles will ever fail to produce good in your life. Therefore, any so-called principle or new method for doing something should always be measured by biblical principles for good stewardship. If it does not comply or attempts to make His instruction null and void, you should not only question it but also refuse to use it.

What good is getting, keeping, and continuing to get more credit when the very principles / methods you've been engaging in have or will get you in trouble in the future and cause you to have trouble over the long haul. In the short haul it may seem a benefit, however looks can be deceiving. There is a way that seems right unto a man, but the end thereof is death.

When you choose the short haul path contrary to biblical instruction, you eventually come to a point in time when that path leads to destruction in the long haul and thereafter even in future short haul periods. Consider the debacle that gripped our economy and individuals over the past few years. Much of it started by unreasonable decisions made concerning housing, real estate, unreasonable mortgage options and selections, the packaging of such mortgages as investments, maxing out loans for cars and personal pleasure merchandise and services, and people throwing diversification of investments and assets out the door.

Individuals and our nation would be in a far better place if we had chosen to apply biblical principles and not be swayed by what looks good in the short haul. We would gain long-term favor and blessing which in turn would positively bless future short-term periods, even though the process would seem hard when first employed. A faithful man shall abound with blessings: but he that makes haste to be rich shall not go unpunished *(Proverbs 28:20)*.

Are you familiar with the term, "don't put all of your eggs in one basket?" This advice was given so if an accident occurs, a majority of eggs would survive and be useable in the future. If you place eggs in several different baskets, you won't drop all the baskets. However, if you place all the eggs in one basket and it crashes to the ground, you chance that many if not all the eggs will be broken.

This concept makes the diversification principle in scripture a most worthwhile principle to include in your wealth building plan. The bible identifies the most important features as giving a portion to seven or eight and using a multitude of counselors to help you manage your life and resources. Yet, many people foolishly put all their savings and investments in one vehicle in one person's or institution's control instead of spreading the risk. They risk the loss of their entire life savings if that one vehicle goes bankrupt or they lose a lot of purchasing power if the value of that one investment vehicle drops substantially.

By diversifying your investments among a variety of counselors *(advisors and saving / investment accounts)*, you eliminate the chance that you will lose your entire life savings. So, for future financial protection, invest your money with at least several reputable counselors and accounts. The accounts can hold investments ranging from stocks to bonds to fixed-income government-guaranteed investments. You will have some risk of loss in value of your holdings no matter what you do. Yet, you should invest in no-load low-expense stock index mutual funds even though they have higher risk of short-term reductions in value than bonds. This risk is worthwhile because historical records have shown the stock market greatly outperforms bonds over long-term periods *(ten consecutive years or more)*. S&P 500, total U.S. stock market, and similar index funds have built-in diversification that protects you by giving you equity ownership in hundreds of profitable businesses.

You can minimize financial risk by:

- Saving for short-term and emergency needs.
- Investing long-term.
- Thoroughly researching and intricately learning the vehicles you choose to invest in.

- Choosing investment vehicles with positive long-term historical track records.

While diversification does not stop investment markets from going up and down or negatively affecting your investments in some short-term periods, it limits the size of such swings on your assets so they won't be anywhere near those for people who had all of their money in the most risky stocks, bonds, real estate, etc. It also allows you to obtain greater overall long-term return than those who put all their money in risk-less fixed-income accounts. In addition, it eliminates the ability of one person to Madoff with all your money.

The bible contains a principle for spreading your risk. Proverbs 11:14 shows there's safety in the multitude of counselors. Ecclesiastes 11:2 exhorts you to give a portion to seven or eight because you don't know what the future may bring. Matthew 25:15 shows the Master giving different amounts of money for investment to three different servants according to their different abilities. Luke 19:13 shows Him giving the same amount to ten different servants. Also, Acts 6:2-3 shows the apostles ordaining seven stewards to oversee the money, resources, and organization that would daily support the widows, orphans, and needy within the Christian community.

I believe these scriptures are trying to let us know that the Holy Spirit encourages, motivates, and guides each person to diversify his/her talent, mind, time, and money in order to get the most out of them and to help protect against inevitable emergencies and catastrophes that will occasionally take place during his/her life. Jesus diversified by choosing twelve very different men with different traits and talents who would work together to share His life with the world. Except for one, Judas, who chose to follow the tempting of satan to become the inevitable catastrophe / emergency that tried to derail the investment He made in the salvation of human souls, the remainder moved forward to become apostles investing gospel seeds in every region of the world they knew about. The plan was not derailed and all we need do is look at the return that continues to be harvested. It started with Jesus investment in twelve different men and now almost half the people on earth name Jesus Christ as their Savior.

This principle flows into the stewardship arena of your life leading you to invest with different financial institutions, brokerage houses, financial counselors, etc. Seven represents completion and is a good number of different types of investment vehicles/accounts to aim for. You will likely start investing with one source *(401k, etc.)* in instruments that diversify like no-load low-expense stock index mutual funds. However, when you properly manage your income and expenses you will soon have extra discretionary cash flow available to invest with another source *(Roth IRA, etc.)*.

Mutual funds provide broad diversification among stocks, bonds, and/or real estate holdings by holding shares of hundreds of different companies. It is a wise decision to build the foundation of your portfolio using several no-load low-expense stock index mutual funds. This minimum level of diversification will give you peace because it greatly enhances the ability of your money to increase with the markets over the long haul and greatly reduces the risk that you might lose a large portion of your investment to unscrupulous counselors or short-term market declines.

Your allocation of investment money should place more of it in vehicles that provide better protection for more of your principle as you get older because as you get older you cannot usually afford to lose great amounts of your money and you may not have time *(10 years or more)* to let the markets work in order to re-grow your assets to adequate levels after a market decline.

In your faith walk, you should take prudent risk which requires godly vision to help carry out your earthly purpose and diversification in the area of saving and investing. Manage your lifestyle and money in a manner that allows you to save and invest a portion of your income equal to a tithe and offering. Such an amount when consistently invested over several decades in a diversified manner with the discipline to forego pulling it out except in extreme emergencies has been shown to provide the kind of wealth that people need to help weather economic storms and provide for them in their latter years.

When you put all your money in one investment account you take the great risk of losing all of it if the investment loses all its value, or the holder thereof goes bankrupt and did not put your money in a segmented account, or if you unknowingly invest with a scam artist running a Ponzi scheme.

These types of things do happen from time to time and they happen in good and bad economic cycles. The principle of diversifying your assets helps protect your asset base from massive and total loss when such things occur. Even though your assets might not earn as much as one particular investment could have earned during a certain period of time, the upside is that you don't have to worry about one bad apple spoiling the whole bunch nor all eggs being broken if you happen to drop the basket.

It has been noted that reasonable asset allocation and diversification have overtime reduced the risk of loss on investment portfolios while at the same time allowing very good growth during long-term investment horizons. Again, the principle of diversification provides greater safety from total loss while rewarding you over the long term with a very reasonable opportunity for meaningful growth of your investments.

Please email me at rparlo@ameritech.net or call 517-393-5081 so I can forward a sample Net Worth Statement and Giving Saving Spending Plan *(budget)* you can use to eliminate financial bondage and powerfully build wealth.

CHAPTER 2

SEVEN FOCUSED STEPS TO FINANCIAL FREEDOM

A sound plan & process based on principles noted above
to eliminate financial bondage and build wealth

Do not live with your eye on this world, rather live with your vision on the world to come. If you hope to become the good steward He instructs you to be and intends for you to be, then you are going to have to develop a deeper fellowship with Jesus Christ through the Holy Spirit that motivates you to follow the pathway the bible lays out for your life and financial health, wealth, and well-being.

Just like Jesus focused all His energies on obtaining the goal of the Father's will for all mankind to have hope of salvation and a heavenly home, you too must focus and take the steps necessary to achieve the Father's goal for you. You should use these steps as your focus to climb the ladder of spiritual financial success one step at a time. Do not attempt to move to the next step until you are firmly established in accomplishing the task on the step you are on, otherwise you will lose the focus and intensity you need to be able *(within the next couple of years)* to become free of consumer debt and get in a much better financial position from which you can build wealth and serve in your calling in a manner that pleases the LORD.

STEP 1: Budget - tell money what to do.

Draft a giving, saving, & spending plan for each month for the next six months. It should identify:

A. Your monthly take home pay *(after-tax income after all payroll deductions are taken out)*.

B. The tithe and offering to be subtracted from take home pay. This is usually calculated as 10+% of your gross income.

C. Each monthly minimum bill payment required by each creditor *(mortgage, rent, car note, phone, internet, natural gas, water & electricity, credit cards, retail charge cards, cable, satellite, streaming services, etc.)*.

D. Other miscellaneous monthly expenses *(groceries, household toiletries, personal money, gas for car, monthly amount of annual property tax payment, monthly amount of annual home and car insurance premium, monthly amount of annual life insurance payment, 2 or 3 low cost weekend vacations each year, low cost monthly entertainment, etc.)*.

E. The surplus or deficit that remains after all expected expenses are accounted for. If there is nothing left over, then you must work with an accountability partner who is good at managing money to determine ways in which you can *(a)* right-size expenses to your current level of income *(shave or eliminate them)*, *(b)* determine which bills receive priority for payment at the current time when you do not have enough to pay them all, and/or *(c)* find work and/or no-cost low-cost entrepreneurial endeavors that will increase your income to get you out of the financial bondage to debt you are in and put you on the road to The Wealthy Place.

If your budget does not show you can achieve financial freedom within the next two years earning the income you do right now and handling expenses like you do right now, then you need to eliminate all: *(a)* non-essential payroll deductions *(unnecessary accident / cancer insurances, etc.)*, *(b)* retirement plan payroll deductions, *(c)* non-essential spending *(eating out, vacations, specialty cable channels, smart phone payments and extras, golf / sports, etc.)* and find other income producing options that allow you to make enough extra money to pay them off in a reasonable time.

You cannot build wealth through irresponsible money management. A lot of money could come into your hands through inheritance or using skills and abilities, yet experience shows it will be foolishly spent and squandered and leave you lacking when you do not handle it according to practical money management principles.

Giving to support Church ministry that builds the LORD's kingdom in the hearts of men is the first step to building true wealth. Knowing the state of your income versus expenses is second. Spending less than your net income is third. Eliminating debt is fourth. Eliminating co-signing is fifth. Saving to cover emergency and purchase desired items is sixth. Making continuous monthly investments is seventh. And, diversification is eighth.

Balancing your checking, savings, investment, and credit accounts each month will help you adhere to the above money management principles so that natural and supernatural abundance can accrue to you. Whereas, failing to *(a)* organize your finances and *(b)* immediately record additions and subtractions to income and expenditures in your accounts will lead to over-spending because you will inevitably think you have more discretionary income than you really have to spend.

Start by balancing your checkbook for the last month at the beginning of each new month by subtracting every check written and all ATM withdrawals from your checkbook balance. Never throw away withdrawal slips until you've balanced your checkbook after the end of each month. Use the balancing method on the back of your monthly statement. If you can't understand the directions, ask a friend or a customer service representative at your financial institution to help you. This process takes about two hours each month but will get easier and less time consuming the more you perform the task and use discretionary income to eliminate debt and creditors from your financial picture.

Now you can use the same type of process to balance your other accounts to ensure *(a)* your monthly expenses are not exceeding your income, *(b)* you're not being charged for items you did not purchase, *(c)* your accounts shows accurate additions and withdrawals for the month, and *(d)* you will contact your financial institution and/ or creditors to straighten out discrepancies. If you are willing and obedient you will reap the rewards of tracking / knowing your income versus expenses. Failing to be a good steward will subject you to future financial harm.

The reality for many people who don't budget is their expenses inevitably outgrow their income and leave them in financial turmoil. You must keep the amount of expenses below the amount of income in order to have financial peace in your life.

It's important to get an income and spending plan *(budget)* started now, because the longer you wait the worse your situation is likely to get. It is not necessary to log every single expense on a ledger for the next few months before you decide what route you must take to correct your situation. You already know your situation is bad and should be better. Simply sit down and figure every expense you're supposed to pay each creditor each month by looking at your bill stubs and checkbook ledger.

Once you've paid the tithe to your local Church, figure the amount you're required to pay each creditor, subtract each amount from your net monthly income as determined by your pay stubs. If you have money left over, this is the amount that you must use to buy personal items, buy groceries, give offerings to fruitful ministries and charities that help other people, and build an emergency fund and later move into investing. If you have little or no money left over, then you need to devise a plan to: reduce the amount of monthly payments you must make; increase your income; reduce the interest rates at which your indebtedness increases; or do all three in order to get your financial house in order and build wealth.

A budget is necessary for successfully managing your finances. Every person should have a budget to ensure they're getting the most out of their income. It helps you see exactly how much comes in versus how much goes out over short-range and long-range periods, so you don't blindly float along buying things and taking on debt that cause your monthly expenses to creep above your monthly net-income.

Without a budget you will likely have no ability to appropriately save and invest for the future. Many people attempt to budget in their heads, but it causes them to fall short on the ability to faithfully pay their bills and meet family needs. Writing out a budget would have forewarned them of the situation and let them know negative consequences would eventually follow if they did not correct the situation.

A computer spreadsheet or online budgeting software makes it easy to write and frequently update a budget. After your initial few hours drafting a budget, you'll only need about an hour each week to maintain it and revise it when necessary to maintain accurate net-income and bill payments.

Show the monthly tithe as the first line item expense and after that list each of your bills including grocery, personal money expenditures, and amounts you want to transfer to emergency funds or savings accounts. The amount left over tells you whether you have a surplus or deficit each month. Now, look at your expense categories to identify each bill payment that can reasonably be eliminated or reduced to help you have a monthly surplus large enough to put toward the tier one $1,000 emergency fund. After that, surplus should be put toward repayment of non-mortgage debt until all loans are paid off. Then, put at least 10% of your gross income into your 401k or another investment account and use the remainder of the surplus to build at least a $10,000 emergency fund. Thereafter, build it to six-months of expenses.

On average it takes people who are focused and diligent *(a)* two to three years to pay off all their non-mortgage debt, *(b)* less than six months thereafter to build the emergency fund to $10,000, and *(c)* about seven years to pay off their mortgage. This happens even while putting more than enough money in their 401k to get the company match. Over the years, budgeting your income and expenses will produce enormous blessings that in the past you never thought possible.

Please email me at rparlo@ameritech.net or call 517-393-5081 so I can forward a sample Net Worth Statement and Giving Saving Spending Plan *(budget)* you can use to eliminate financial bondage and powerfully build wealth.

STEP 2: Build a $1,000 first-tier emergency fund.

When you have non-mortgage debt you must pay off, use all surplus that remains at the end of each month to build an emergency fund equal to at least $1,000. This will help you stop turning to credit cards and loans to take care of problems and emergencies. You will get on the right path to using cash instead of burdening your future with debt.

This money should be put in a savings or money market account that can be accessed quickly when an emergency occurs. You could build your emergency fund to a higher amount if you know you will experience a more costly expense several months down the road *(layoff, large uncovered medical bill, etc.)*.

Emergencies will occur at various times in life and you need to be as financially prepared for them as you can be. The drafting of your monthly budgets should let you know the amount of surplus money after minimum expense payments are made. This can be put toward quickly building a $1,000 emergency fund. Then after repayment of all non-mortgage debt *(credit cards, car loans, personal loans)*, use the surplus money *(which is larger now due to less expense payments)* to build a $10,000 emergency fund and thereafter build it to at least six-months of expenses, so you never have to return to financial bondage by borrowing money when emergencies occur. Whenever you must spend the funds below $10,000, then you should reduce discretionary spending and surplus debt payments and /or pursue extra entrepreneurial ventures to bring in extra income until you once again build the fund back to an appropriate level. Stopping debt repayment / elimination for a short period of time during economic downturns will not hurt your progress when you have appropriate emergency funds to cover your lifestyle and business basics. If a downturn occurs and you do not have an emergency fund, then you risk foreclosure, bankruptcy, and other non-payment ramifications like loss of business, property, goods, etc.

On average it takes people who are focused *(a)* two to three months to build the $1,000 emergency fund, *(b)* two to three years to pay off non-mortgage debt, *(c)* about three months thereafter to build the emergency fund to $10,000, *(d)* another three months to build the emergency fund to cover six-months of expenses, and *(e)* about seven years to pay off a home mortgage, even while putting the minimum amount of money in a 401k that enables them to get the company match. Over the years, budgeting your income and expenses will produce enormous blessings that in the past you never thought could be realized.

Certainly, it's not wrong to want things nor to have things. Yet, when expenses consistently exceed income, your lifestyle puts you in financial bondage. Likewise, when you do not have substantial assets to produce income to provide for you and family during periods of low or no income, your monthly loan payments will be your downfall. You must learn that all things come in time – the right time; when the LORD has provided for you in such a way that you are able to, without debt, purchase the things you desire while maintaining a healthy emergency fund and growing asset base that will be able to provide income for your retirement / re-fire-ment years so you can pursue your passions *(ministry, entrepreneurial efforts, etc.)* while enjoying the type of comfort you will need during your senior years.

When the time for investing occurs at step 4 of the plan, you will be able to invest on a long-term basis *(largely in no-load low-expense broad stock index mutual funds that fluctuate from day to day or year to year)* without pulling your money out of such investments due to fear when the market declines because you built an emergency fund to cover monthly expenses when emergency situations occur.

Having more than enough money to do all the LORD called you to do will be an intricate part of living an abundant life on Earth. He does not want you poor, broke, and in financial turmoil. Therefore, the Holy Spirit gave principles for good stewardship. He desires that we pursue lifestyles and character that employ it. No matter your current level of income or assets, the following simple steps will discipline you, ready you for His work, let you know He is your source, and help you make His will the first priority in your life.

You should put emergency funds in financial institution accounts guaranteed by FDIC or NCUA because safety and the ability to withdraw the whole amount at any time is what you need in case you encounter an emergency for which you need this money *(uncovered medical expense, layoff, extended unemployment, etc.)*. Never keep more than $250,000 in any one bank or credit union, because no matter how many different accounts it holds for you that is all that is guaranteed to be reimbursed per person if that financial institution is liquidated. If you have far more than that amount there are some financial institutions that can collaborate with one another to assign your funds to each of the institutions in a way that will provide protection for all your money.

The LORD's return is imminent. It's certainly closer today than it has ever been and He instructs us that upon His return, we should be found busy completing our part of the Great Commission in our family, workplaces, neighborly relationships, and all arenas of life. We are citizens of Heaven and need to understand we are seated with Jesus Christ in heavenly places, yet we should not be so heavenly minded that we are no earthly good. Thus, we must understand that biblical principles require natural actions we are empowered by Him to take. This often brings supernatural results that glorify Him and produces the good He intends for you and others.

Prayer brings great results that we desperately need in our lives and world, yet it must be displayed by the work of opening your heart, mind, ears, and mouth to listen for the LORD and talk with Him. Reading the scripture on a regular basis like we should, or with any regularity, requires that we actually open the book, use the internet, or some other physical tool to distinguish the LORD's instruction in order to progressively know what is important to Him and for you and other people. Thus, you should recognize that He instructs everyone to take action in the financial and other arenas of our lives that are physical in nature and are good works that bring supernatural results when employed. Saving is one of these principles that require action that you do not want to overlook or think He does not care about lest you fail to receive the great benefits that He stored therein for your life, care of your family, and future involvement with the ministry of the Church to change the lives and trajectories of many other people for His glory.

Proverbs lets us know that a fool quickly spends all he / she receives whereas the wise save for the future. Scripture indicates a wise person would not build a house without counting the cost to know he / she has enough to complete it. A reasonable amount of savings and an ongoing pattern of saving a portion of the money the LORD entrusts to you helps you solidly build the house of your life and maintain stable financial footing while you move deeper into the life and work He called you to.

People that employ a give first, save next, and spend third habit in their financial lives more often have a greater positive impact in life than those whose habit is to spend, spend, spend. Usually, believers who master this principle give abundantly to ministry work and their tithes and offerings grow larger throughout the future. It's almost impossible to consistently give as the LORD instructs and have something to invest for future growth unless you first live beneath your income and save because the desire for things of this world and massive debt to get them otherwise encompass a greater part of your income and stops you. This brings unnecessary sorrow into your life by stopping the natural and supernatural flow of blessing He intends for you and your family. Our LORD is all about helping you eliminate unnecessary sorrow and having maximum impact throughout the course of your life and He determined that this could not be done without consistently employing saving as a financial component of your life.

STEP 3: Pay off all non-mortgage debt as quickly as possible.

Chances are these credit cards, car loans, personal loans, etc. charge interest that is well above what you can earn in savings or MMAs. Thus, after you have built the $1,000 emergency fund, you should use the monthly surplus to pay the next smallest debt and so on until you have finally paid off all your debts. The only time you break this cycle is when you have an emergency that needs immediate attention and you must expend money in your emergency fund to take care of it. Then, you would rebuild your emergency fund with the monthly surplus and afterward resume paying down your debt with it.

The Debt Avalanche and Debt Snowball methods are viable for eliminating debts in the shortest possible time. Clearly, His desire is that you not be a debtor. He blessed us with wisdom that would help us avoid loans and other forms of indebtedness. In order for this wisdom to benefit us, we must choose to walk down His path for our lives versus the path that the enemy wants to lure us down through the examples and advice of worldly men who load themselves down with debt and encourage us to do the same.

When using the Avalanche method, you pay only the minimum due on all bills except the one with the highest finance charge and the lowest balance. Place all extra money on this account each pay period until it is paid off. Now, add the monthly payment and all extra money to the minimum payment for the account next in line that now has the highest finance charge and the lowest balance.

When using the Snowball method, you pay only the minimum due on all bills except the one with the smallest overall balance. Place all extra money on this account each pay period until it is paid off. Now, add the monthly payment and all extra money to the minimum payment for the account next in line that now has the smallest balance.

Continue using the approach until all debt is paid off and remember to close each account and cut up the associated credit card once the debt is eliminated. This debt-reduction method works best when you discipline yourself to refuse to take on debt that you cannot immediately pay off in full. Choose not to use credit to purchase anything you do not have cash available right now to cover, except for a house purchase at a reasonable amount in comparison to your stable yearly income and overall wealth.

You could augment this process by shopping for accounts that charge less interest than your current accounts in order to transfer as much higher interest debt as possible to the lower interest accounts. Also, you could use a low interest home equity loan to pay off credit card and other consumer debt. Be aware that many credit card, consumer loan, and home equity loan interest rates are variable and could go up and become problematic if at any time interest rates rise substantially, if the variable rate is periodically set by the financial institution using an unstable interest rate index, or if the contract allows the financial institution to raise the interest rate when you fail to make timely payment. Therefore, if you use these methods to transfer debt you must be disciplined and committed to paying off the new account(s) as quickly as possible, otherwise your home could be taken from you or other grave consequences could befall you if you fail to make monthly loan payments as laid out in the contract(s).

The Avalanche will get the best financial impact because you will pay less interest to creditors and more quickly eliminate debt. However, the snowball method provides the psychological boost most people need in the beginning of their journey because the quick wins of paying off a couple of debts in a short time period motivates them to continue to pay off loans and stay out of debt.

Types of debt most people encounter are: Home mortgages; Second mortgages; Home Equity loans; Vehicle loans; Student loans; Credit card loans; Store charge card loans; and Business loans. Most debt is bad and all types of debt can put you in financial harm's way when you take on unreasonable amounts and do not quickly seek to get yourself out of it. Most people have a skill or ability that can bring them enough income to progressively move out of poverty if they properly manage the income and their lifestyle and pursue investment avenues that build wealth. Many medical providers and hospitals often provide pro bono or low-cost ways to get life-saving surgery and Churches and charities provide huge amounts of food and delicately used goods people can glean when needed. This also helps people avoid loans.

Worshipping at the altar of debt in order to maintain good credit scores by continually taking on more debt is not working for most people. The absolute best approach you can take to obtain financial freedom is to employ a singular focus and stop spraying in numerous directions trying to do a whole lot of things that are not helpful. It is futile to think you're going to be a good investor earning high returns when you cannot manage the current income entrusted to you, which you show by lacking a reasonable emergency fund and barely being able to pay your bills or worse. It is likewise futile to believe you can maintain a high credit score by taking on more debt or when you are entertaining deficit spending in your monthly budgets. Need I say, like the Robot to Will Robinson, while frantically waving my arms hoping you get the point, "Danger Will Robinson, Danger, Danger, Danger Will Robinson!"

Intense focus on NOT taking on additional debt along with total debt elimination and maintaining a debt-free life is the process

/ good stewardship lifestyle that make it possible for you to be what He wants: debt-free, in a financially sound and asset rich position instead of the poverty-stricken position of a borrower. He wants you to release yourself from slavery *(bondage)* to lenders and to owe no one anything but love. This enables you to carry out His call and purpose for you to evangelize and make disciples of other people and have greater monetary means to help meet the needs of widows, orphans, and those poor & oppressed.

STEP 4: Invest at least 10% of your gross income each pay period.

Once all non-mortgage debts are paid off, invest at least 10% of your gross income. Make sure you put into your 401k the percentage of pay necessary to get the full amount of your employer's match.

Put the money in a safe and sound investment *(like a stable value account)* until you study and understand the history, nature, risk, and investment costs / fees of other types of investments like stocks, bonds, mutual funds, real estate, etc. Pretty quickly, you will likely draw the conclusion that the greater portion of your investment money should be put in no-load low-expense total stock market index mutual funds or equivalent funds. You will also likely conclude that a smaller portion could be put in no-load low-expense intermediate length bond index mutual funds and equivalent funds that pay higher interest than you can get from bank certificates of deposit.

Historical investment returns are not a guarantee of future returns, these types of funds generally provide the right amount of risk, reward, and safety over the long-term horizon. The breadth of companies each one invests in and the seven or so different investment accounts one will hold over time *(per the diversification principle)* usually result in one never running into a scenario where a market depression, recession, correction, or downturn reduces holdings to anywhere near zero dollars. Investors periodically experience stock value *(price)* reductions but the market has roared back each time in 18-months on average and restored overall stock market value above the amount it was at prior to each downturn.

Save at least 10 percent of your income throughout your work years in seven or eight reliable equity investment vehicles that are easy to understand, that contain broad diversification, and that have historically netted higher reliable long-term returns. The best assets to own as a bulk of your portfolio is a diversified portfolio of company stock via no-load low-expense stock index mutual funds mimicking the S&P 500 or the total stock market. Over time, you should buy stock ownership via at least 4 or 5 mutual funds from different fund families *(Vanguard, Fidelity, Charles Schwab, TIAA-CREF, American Funds, etc.)* along with your 3 or more bank or credit union savings, money market, and/or CD accounts that contain your emergency funds, other sinking funds for future planned purchases *(cars, home renovations, travel, etc.)*, and short-term income withdrawals.

Stock mutual funds have more historical data that show consistently larger positive grow trends over a consecutive ten year and greater investing cycles than any other type of investment. a 25 to 30% portion of investible assets can be put in stable value funds and/or no-load low-expense intermediate bond index mutual funds, when people believe they need short-term protection from stock market temporary downturns. One should take into account that the average number of years in which most market downturns correct themselves and go higher than the previous high is about two years. So, most money invested in the market would be safe as long as you only have to or choose to withdraw four to five percent from your accounts in any year. You will be better off waiting for downturns to subside and for growth to take off once again when you do not let emotions overtake you.

Other assets *(e.g. investment real estate, antique cars, etc.)* could be worthwhile but usually require more skill to purchase, properly maintain, and appropriately manage, and accurately determine annual average growth patterns. In addition, they might not provide much risk protection and investing stability when you cannot own enough of them to truly be diversified. Thus, it is recommended that you build the first-tier emergency fund, then eliminate your non-mortgage debts, then build the emergency fund to at least $10,000 before you begin investing ten percent of your gross income. The only caveat being you may want to start investing earlier when your employer gives you a generous 401k match and you still have enough discretionary income to eliminate your debt within the next few years.

The benefit to using federally regulated 401k, 403b, and 457 investment plans offered by your employer is that a portion of your earned income can be placed in these plans on a tax deferred basis. You pay no income taxes on this money until you withdraw money from the account. Federal regulations allow employers to let you to invest about $20,000 annually through each plan and the IRS increases that maximum each year. These accounts generally include an array of choices such as fixed interest vehicles and stock and bond investments that automatically diversify your investment holdings.

It is costly to withdraw money from any of these plans until you are age 59 and a half. This keeps you from squandering all your money in your peak earning years so you have a chance at building wealth you'll need to maintain comfort in senior years. If taken before then *(except through a loan from the plan administrator that you pay back on schedule)* you must pay income taxes on the money and a 10% penalty to the IRS. If money is withdrawn after qualified early retirement or on an equal periodic payment basis per federal code 72t, no penalty is due but you must still pay federal, state, and city income tax on the withdrawn money.

There are borrowing options, but we do not recommend them because you'll pay the loan in after tax dollars and those dollars will be taxed again when you withdraw it in later years. In addition, if you lose your job or are laid off or leave for any reason, you will have to pay income taxes and the 10% penalty on the outstanding loan amount because it cannot be paid back through your employer's payroll system.

Mutual funds provide broad diversification among stocks and/or bonds. Some have initial investment requirements of a few thousand dollars. However, some allow investors to bypass such requirements when they authorize monthly electronic fund transfers of as little as $50 from a bank account.

If you can't or don't wish to use this option, you should quickly save the required amount to invest in a mutual fund with a good reputation, good historical returns, and low expense ratio. Checking these items is less difficult for mutual funds than for individual stocks, bonds, and other investments. Your state securities regulator can let you know if a fund is reputable and the fund's prospectus will display one-year, five-year, ten-year, and lifetime average annual returns as well as the fund's expense ratio.

Large, medium, and small cap index funds are great choices when you aren't sure how to identify acceptable returns or select funds based on the credentials of the portfolio manager. Index funds will provide you with a long-term average annual return that is commensurate with overall stock market returns for these categories of businesses.

As you learn more about investing, in an attempt to obtain higher returns, you could choose to invest in funds whose portfolio of stocks and/or bonds is based on a non-index fund objective and manager's stock selection preferences. You should utilize trustworthy financial advisors to help analyze your family's need for different types of funds. This should include discussion about how you can reasonably revise your budget to cover required expense payments, investment amounts, and other alternatives.

Many people get laid off, receive less pay, and have their overall assets reduced during times of stock market correction, recession, and depression. One has only to review the history of the U.S. and world economies to recognize that these times will come. Yet, by failing to save, invest, and live in accordance with biblical principles many people act as if they're oblivious to the fact that these economic situations will arise at some point.

Unfortunately, most people engage in personal money management practices that will land them in financial turmoil at some point in their lives, especially when several of the major markets are down, such as stock and real estate. Turmoil occurs because they continue to do things the world's way like taking on ever increasing debt to purchase material things beyond the reach of their current income and assets. Many also fail to honor the LORD by tithing to spread the gospel of Jesus Christ and minister to others. At the same time, others spend all their resources on get- rich-quick business ventures and supposed high-earning investment schemes marketed by people whose promises turn out to be untrustworthy.

They fail to realize that you cannot listen to anyone who tells you a specific investment method or type of business is successful for everyone who uses it. The only time you want to listen and obey such advice is when the bible says all believers should follow specific principles or methods such as diligently performing a god-pleasing type of work, tithing, spending far less than 89% of your gross pay, saving, investing, eliminating current debt, and refusing to take on future debt, etc.

Otherwise, the heavy concentration you make in one investment or industry will usually turn into a financial downfall for you, especially when you do not become an expert in how that market operates in hopes of avoiding downturns or accumulating enough income and assets to weather storms. When you engage in such risky get-rich-quick endeavors you will suffer foreclosure, bankruptcy, unrecoverable losses, and/or great discomfort for a lengthy time in order to get back to the place where He wanted you to be all along.

He provides preventative maintenance instructions by putting investment principles in the bible that help us overcome the severe effects of economic downturn. This doesn't mean that you'll never be touched by storms or that you should take no business or investment risks. Every person will face obstacles and catastrophes in life and every investment carries the risk that it may not grow and that the investor might lose principal. However, you always have a better chance of maintaining your lifestyle, giving, saving, investing, and recovering losses when you consistently make two actions part of your financial plan:

1. Diligently work to get out and stay out of debt by regularly paying down and ultimately paying off everything from credit card debt to car loans to home mortgages.
2. Diversify assets by buying seven or eight different types of investments.

These principles help you overcome the downturns that affect every investment market. Historically, down markets do not affect every industry or investment at the same time, so using these two principles allows you to be in a place where you're not negatively affected or moved by current economic winds. You can spend whatever income you receive to meet your needs without having bill collectors chasing you to pay debts you cannot afford. Also, you have a much greater possibility of annual asset growth when only a few markets are down at the same time because the growth of investments you have in markets that are up have an opportunity to outweigh the losses you will experience in markets that are down.

As you can see, He provides insulation against economic upheaval, but you must do your part to employ His plan so you are always in a position where you can come out ahead no matter what economic / financial obstacles come your way.

If your finances are not in a position to purchase the tools you really need to protect your family, this is the perfect time to utilize your advisors to help develop a plan that will help you take action to put your finances in shape so that you can have more than enough money at some point in the future to fund the tools you really need.

No matter how much you are able to purchase, always stand

on the fact He will take care of you and give you peace to guard your heart and mind in situations you can't currently provide for or control. He is your only ironclad protection. However, never let this stop you from being a good steward who uses the financial tools you can to help protect your family from the risks that everyone faces in this life.

STEP 5: Build your emergency fund to at least $10,000.

After all non-mortgage debts are paid off and you have initiated putting 10% of gross income into investments *(via 401k or brokerage accounts)* use monthly surplus *(which is much larger than when you began using these steps)* to build your emergency fund to at least $10,000. Again, you could build your emergency fund to a higher amount if you know you will experience a more costly expense several months down the road *(layoff, large uncovered medical bill, etc.)*.

After you pay off all non-mortgage debt, build your emergency fund to a minimum $10,000 and seek to maintain it, so when an emergency occurs you do not return to financial bondage by having to borrow money and pay interest, taxes, IRS penalties, and other fees. Emergency fund money should only be spent for unforeseen emergencies that require you to spend money to resolve them. Emergencies will occur at various times in life and you need to be as prepared for them as you can be. At this point in the process you will have plenty of discretionary cash flow left over *(because all non-mortgage debts are paid off)* to quickly build your emergency fund to $10,000. Build your emergency fund larger when $10,000 does not approximate three to six months of basic expenses for your household.

You might also need to build a larger emergency fund if you know you will soon face an emergency *(layoff, large uncovered medical expense, etc.)* and will need to cover it as well as household expenses. In addition, build a larger emergency fund when you're in an industry where pay is uncertain and/or unequal from month to month or year to year *(construction, consulting, etc.)*.

As you can see, $10,000 is only being used as an easier means to envision and get to the larger emergency fund target at this point in the Seven Step Plan. For most people who pay off everything but their mortgage this amount would equate to about three months of household expenses. The emergency fund you ultimately decide to build is not a one size fits all number, but you should seek to ensure coverage for three to six months of household expenses plus one-time expenses you estimate you would incur during a period of emergency. On average it takes people who are focused less than a few years to pay off all their consumer debt, and less than six months thereafter to build the emergency fund to $10,000.

Usually, this money should be put in financial institution accounts guaranteed by FDIC or NCUA because safety and the ability to withdraw the whole amount at any time is what you need in case you encounter an emergency for which you need this money *(uncovered medical expense, layoff, extended unemployment, etc.)*. This money is not intended to be investments, rather insurance against negative things happening that bring financial costs and need to cover expenses that your usual monthly income cannot handle.

Be aware that no financial institution should have more than $250,000 of your money because this is the maximum amount guaranteed per institution by the FDIC or NCUA according to federal law, no matter the number of different accounts you might hold it in.

You could consider putting some of the emergency fund in money market mutual funds managed by brokerage houses like Vanguard, Fidelity, Charles Schwab, TIAA, etc. They tend to be very conservative and safe in investing practices and protecting principle and earnings and work much like the bank savings accounts. The interest they pay is also in a similar range. They do not have a federal guarantee that principle / dollar value could not go down and thus they are a bit different than bank and credit union guarantees. The

SIPC insures brokerage investments up to $500,000 against loss caused by mismanagement, malfeasance, theft, and other situations. Again, it does not guarantee you will not lose principle / dollar value based on market swings at any given time. That's why I would not put all emergency funds in this type of account. Also, I believe so heavily in diversification as a God-given saver / investor protection that I would put portions of larger emergency funds into several different institutions, so it is not all in one basket.

Your aim should be to live debt-free and use the emergency fund to help you get through several years of unemployment or disability if a long-lasting emergency or catastrophe were to occur. Also, to place such funds, that will be used to pay usual periodic bills and other needs, in accounts that provide good guarantees of return of principle and earned interest. In addition, if you were to spend the funds below $10,000, then you should reduce discretionary spending and surplus debt payments and /or pursue extra entrepreneurial ventures to bring in extra income until you once again build the fund back to an appropriate level.

STEP 6: Pay off mortgage debt.

After you have saved the larger emergency fund per the last step. Use monthly surplus to eliminate your mortgage. It many instances, it could be eliminated within seven years from the date you engage this step.

Commit to not purchasing another house until at least 5 to 7 years after you have paid off your current mortgage so that you give yourself plenty of time to enjoy a couple of thrills paid for with a bit of your surplus cash. Also, this gives you time to save and invest a portion of surplus cash to exponentially expand your portfolio for retirement, missions, and passions. If you have a desire to purchase another home, set the purchase as a faith goal to pursue on a debt-free basis using the equity in your current home and savings you are able to build each month after your current home mortgage is paid off. Remember contentment and deferred gratification pay off more in the end than encumbering yourself further in debt.

You should consider selling rental properties early in the process to use the equity to more quickly become debt-free, especially when properties are not returning great profits each month after expenses and they are causing a cash flow crisis in your finances.

Those who offer financial guidance that does not conform with biblical principles have ensnared many people in destructive practices that seemed like they would be fruitful, profitable, and prosperous when employed. Yet, many people have found they do not work and are destructive to the mindset and discipline they should employ and thus have actually harmed their finances. Some tell people they should never pay off a mortgage because of the tax break they receive and the return they can earn on investments using money that would have gone toward paying off the mortgage. Scripture shows it is always better to be out of debt than in debt and we should be ever working to get to and maintain a debt-free lifestyle. Do you believe the LORD or do you believe man?

There have been millions of instances of people going bankrupt and experiencing home / property foreclosures, vehicle repossessions, and incessant bill collector calls. This shows that He knows better than everyone else the ills of carrying debt, especially over the long term. These negative consequences of debt never had to happen. People who get to the point of managing their income to live well beneath their means and those who get to the point of living debt-free no longer experience these negative results because they owe no one anything but love.

Another thing that is often not shared with those being advised is that the vast majority of people will never develop the steely long-term attitude, emotions, and investment know-how to be able to out earn the interest rate they pay on their mortgages. In fact, most of those dishing out such advice will never be able to do this either. Unfortunately, most people start buying equity shares when prices are high based on the emotion that anybody can make money owning them and then they sell them off at a lower price because they experience a market decline that they cannot emotionally and mentally handle.

Add to that the fact that there is always a small percentage of advisors who only want to make money off of people and thus will motivate clients to frequently move from one commission paying investment to another *(churning accounts)* in order to make as much money as possible, all while making the client feel that such moves are in the client's best interest.

In some instances, harmful financial advice comes from advisors that are famous, rich, powerful, and/or successful in the eyes of their clients. It can also come from advisors with professional designations behind their names and those with long and influential track records who rub elbows with the investing elite *(remember Madoff)*. It can also be dished out by people who are spiritually influential *(pastors, preachers, televangelists, etc.)*.

People continue to be coerced into poor financial decisions by messages that point out all the material things they do not have and are made to feel like second-class citizens when they don't keep up with the Joneses. Many are made to feel that they cannot be happy if they do not obtain the same things and the same types of positions as those that society considers successful. The result of believing and following worldly advice and operating with the wrong motives produces extremely negative results. No wonder many people suffer more than they have to when economic downturn cycles come and no wonder societies create economic downturns that never had to take place.

You should never follow a course of action, financial or otherwise, without studying the bible to see if it is aligned with His will and thus is pleasing to Him. You should also consider whether the guidance, at any point in time, would cause you to engage in activities that keep you from regular fellowship with Him and His people *(the Church)*. Otherwise, you will fail to plant and water the gospel in your and other people's lives, build them up in the faith, and be the good example He wants you to be.

Most people who dish out or follow ungodly advice lack peace, joy, and fulfillment in this life no matter what it seems like to other people and no matter the testimonial they give to others. Remember, the devil would have you believe his minions are living a better life than the one He planned for you. We know this is not true. When you follow the devil's guidance you reap the consequences meant for him. This has unfortunately led millions of people into godless and unwise pursuit of material things that resulted in repossessions, bankruptcies, foreclosures, and other spiritual, mental, emotional, and physical ills.

Some people seem to gain opulent material things and prominence among men in this life, but they will be insignificant and unsuccessful in the LORD's eyes and will suffer a devastating eternal fate because they do not adhere to His will by asking for His wisdom, living within His commands, and employing His lifestyle and financial principles. Rightly divide the Word of Truth, so you can experience His blessings and rewards and help others understand what they need to do to receive them.

He desires debt-freedom for your personal life and business ownership. Many have ignored His instructions and warnings about debt and others have compromised His standards not believing it is possible to be debt-free. While a few people appearing better off because they leveraged debt, the vast majority of people destroy long-term peace and joy in their lives by taking on excessive debt.

I believe there are a few legitimate reasons for taking on debt.

1. Parents with no way to provide food and/or shelter during a period of poverty in which severe hardship has overtaken the family.
2. A person who has liquid assets with a dollar value that covers the total loan plus interests and costs and also has enough stable income / cash flow to cover the monthly payments and

pay it off early. This scenario includes real estate purchases for a primary home, rental property, flipping, or commercial property.

The latter type of indebtedness *(real estate purchase)* is considered shrewd by some people because the asset may increase in value to be far greater than the outstanding amount of the loan and because renting the property may create enough cash flow *(income)* to more than cover the monthly loan payment and any other expenses resulting from ownership of the assets. In such situations, you earn more on your money than you pay out in interest on the loan. Some call it using the world's money to make a fortune for the kingdom.

However, you must be careful in considering this option because many people overestimated the property values, income earning ability, cash flow and underestimated possible negative effects when things do not go as planned *(repossession, foreclosure, bankruptcy, ulcers, etc.)*. Many people with good intentions have been unable to produce enough cash flow to cover loan payments. In some instances, the value of the properties dropped due to market conditions to an amount below what is owed on the loan*(s)*. Many people *(including Christians)* were forced to file bankruptcy or had properties foreclosed on and wound up with huge amounts of debt still being pursued by bill collectors and in some cases the government.

When people compromise by taking on debt instruments without the net worth to cover the entire amount of indebtedness, they usually shortchange the Kingdom of God and the Church and bring financial hardship upon their families because they often stop tithing and giving abundantly to further the Great Commission we are told to support. Our giving brings great reward. Unfortunately, for many people, one bad choice seems to never be enough, so they enter into more situations with other creditors for mortgages, car notes, charge cards, student loans, business loans, etc. This drastically reduces and/or eliminates discretionary income that could be used to invest and grow wealth and puts them in a position where they choose to pay creditors instead of putting Jesus Christ first while leading people to Him and teaching them how to walk in His will.

While most people want blessings and rewards from the LORD, they unfortunately make financial pacts with the devil and give his methods more allegiance than they give biblical principles. Your vision should be focused on the fact that He is able to prosper you and grow great wealth for your family without you getting into debt. He wants to bring you out of debt, not further encumber your life with debt. Debt freedom along with wealth building is truly the best financial position to work yourself into. It's wonderful to know we have Almighty God whose vision for you is that large and who is powerful enough to help you make it happen!

Many people try to hold onto houses with mortgages currently above their ability to bear because being in them makes it look to other people like they have arrived *(reached a coveted socio-economic status or they are living the life)*. Some have done the same thing with commercial and industrial property. Don't let the American Dream become your American Nightmare.

I know many people whom He showed how to manage income according to biblical principles long before their supervisors promoted them at work. In a few short years they systematically eliminated debts and were well on their way to becoming wealthy way beyond what they could naturally envision a few years earlier. Some moved on to start successful businesses. They could not count on employers or customers to increase their wages / revenue, or do anything special for them financially. They chose to rely on the LORD's plan to make them fruitful, profitable, and prosperous via their willingness to properly manage the lives, money, and relationships entrusted to them.

Home ownership is usually touted as the foundation for and means for all Americans to build wealth. However, irresponsible home buyers *(those misinformed about the costs of home ownership above the monthly payment, and those who move to higher cost homes every*

5 to 10 years) are generally in financial bondage like irresponsible renters. They purchased more home than they can truly afford for many years to come. Not to mention, many of their mortgages are severely under water - they owe far more to the financial institutions that hold them than the homes are worth and they cannot easily and quickly sell them and get out of even a portion of the bondage.

It is not automatically true that owning a home makes you wealthier or will do so in the future. Believing this lie and acting upon it without first counting the true cost of home ownership and debt freedom will cost you dearly as it has many millions of people in the past. Believing the lie will move you to do anything to get a house like accepting predatory lending terms with high interest rates and costs. It will also lead you to believe you can afford what the banks say you can afford rather than you making an honest assessment of your finances, so you know what you can truly afford while building and maintaining a large emergency fund cushion to handle unforeseen home ownership costs and other emergency life situations requiring large outlays of cash.

Home ownership can be great when you truly can afford the home you are going to purchase. It can bring peace from apartment neighbors making noise bouncing off the walls and it could provide more space to entertain friends. Yet, for many millions of people it is not as financially fantastic as the pundits make it seem.

The 10-35% federal income tax deduction that one may be able to use with regard to mortgage interest / property tax payments is only useful to the extent that your itemized deductions are greater than the standard deduction for your filing status. Also, you must remember that every year throughout your ownership of the house you will pay thousands of dollars in property taxes to your local governments for which you may only get a fraction of a discount via federal taxes or homestead credits. In addition, all the maintenance, repairs, and renovations will not bring greater return for most people given the amount of principle and interest they will pay on the loans they acquire to do these things.

You should say "NO" if I offered you the great deal of giving me $10,000, so I can return to you only $1,000 to $3,500. Think of the tax deduction for mortgage interest and property taxes in the same way, so you are totally sober and realistic regarding what you have been told are benefits of homeownership. It is always best to have absolutely no debt and the cash needed to purchase a property outright. This alone would help people be much more reasonable about the property they would seek to purchase.

However, if you believe home ownership is worth obtaining a loan to make it a reality then you should follow a few simple rules:

1. Pay off all other debt, build at least six months of income as an emergency reserve and also put away enough money in savings to make a 20% down payment at closing.

2. Inventory your work / business environment to ensure you are not subject to bouts of unemployment or wild swings that would lower monthly income within the few years leading up to and after a house purchase. Remember, approximately 100% of foreclosures are a result of the purchasers' inability to continue paying the mortgages and/or property taxes.

3. Look to buy a property in a community where history of ownership shows steady price appreciation over the last 10 to 20 years, unless the Holy Spirit has spoken that you should move to a specific community for ministry purposes, etc.

4. Only obtain a low interest 15-year fixed rate mortgage and seek to have enough in extra discretionary income that you can pay it off much sooner than 15 years.

5. Put at least 20% down.

6. Do not purchase any property where the monthly payment of principle, interest, property tax, and insurance would require more than 28% of your monthly gross income.

If you prudently act to do these things you will find that home ownership will be very kind and good for you and eventually lead to paying lower housing costs than being a long-term renter and this will give you extra discretionary income that you can use to invest and build wealth according to scriptural design.

Remember, home ownership is not the key to wealth building and being a renter is not a disadvantage. Biblical-based wealth building is accomplished by *(a)* honoring the LORD, *(b)* continually keeping your monthly expenses well under your monthly net income, *(c)* becoming debt-free, and *(d)* investing discretionary cash flow over long periods of time *(5, 10, 20 years, etc.)*. Even with promotions and entrepreneurial endeavors that become lucrative over time, you must still do the above to really excel at wealth building that releases you from bondage and provides financial freedom when measured against extraordinary income earned. For example, a net worth of $5 million dollars for a person who earns $2 million per year and spends all his take-home pay will last approximately 2.5 years if his income stopped coming in.

A lifestyle that moves you to eliminating all debt, including mortgages, always betters your long-term financial condition because it positions you to always be able to honor the LORD with your tithes and offerings so Heaven's windows are open over you.

Some financial advisors tell people it is not good to pay off a current mortgage because you can make more money by investing in the stock market or by leveraging your money to obtain more loans to get investment real estate and the monthly rental payments they believe will come from it. However, this is tricky at best because even with investment advice most people are not good enough investors to be able to get greater annual investment return than the interest charged on their mortgage*(s)*.

Financial advisors have their place and reputable ones can be consulted to help educate you to be a responsible manager of the money entrusted to you and to help you maintain emotional composure and reasonable investment allocation / diversification when the economic environment looks good, bad, or indifferent over short and long periods of time. However, you should not use them because you believe they have the ability to pick the greatest investments and guarantee gains on investments. For good reason the SEC requires investment firms to put the following type of statement on their investment literature, "Past investment returns are no guarantee of future investment results."

In addition, most people are simply not good landlords and managers of rental property or good at fixing up and flipping properties and so they lose money on these investment choices and find that over the years they are not in a better financial position than if they had simply paid off their mortgage and saved and reasonably invested over the course of the years of their lives. The problem is exacerbated when the properties are not within close proximity to where they live.

Again, people are often told by financial advisors, accountants, and tax preparers that they should keep their mortgages because of the tax deduction / reduction the interest payments afford them each year. However, only about 40% of people with mortgages itemize their federal tax returns and thus get a reduction in taxes owed. Even with housing expenses, the others did not spend enough to surpass the standard deduction.

I understand that part of the benefit you may get from a mortgage is the ability to be in a house that you want right now with the price locked in. However, that does not make it smart to continue paying mortgage interest when you could in fact pay off the mortgage. Rapidly paying off your mortgage builds the right kind of discipline. Most people will never make or maintain funding investment when they do not first employ rapid mortgage debt reduction plans. Any extra money they get is usually spent on frivolous stuff they cannot remember a few years down the road.

You will lift a great debt burden off your shoulders and will feel extreme freedom and will have removed the possibility that you could one day be in a situation where a financial institution is foreclosing on the home(s) you have made monthly payments on for so long. You can at the point of mortgage payoff begin saving what was your monthly mortgage payment and then not have to worry about whether or not you can actually earn more than the mortgage interest amount.

You are also free to take extra investment risk with a portion of the money if you choose to do so without running into the possibility that you may one day owe financial institutions money that you cannot pay them. This type of financial freedom relieves stress and pressure and puts you in a position where the LORD can entrust you with far more money and resources because you have proven to be a good steward whose eyes and actions are on Him and His way rather than the way of the world.

Eliminating debt and being debt-free for ten, twenty, or more years will usually afford you with hundreds of thousands and sometimes millions of dollars more of assets that you get the gains from and use of in order to properly care for your family, fund the gospel, pursue your God-given purpose, and enjoy good things without being stressed out and pressed out. Therefore, paying off loans including home loans always makes sense, so you are not ensnared by the awful consequences of debt that can so quickly overtake you when you least expect it, like not being able to make loan payments due to loss of income resulting from loss of job contracts, loss of customers, disability, layoff, economic downturn, recession, depression, downturn, coronavirus, etc.

STEP 7: Give more abundantly, build greater wealth, and spend more.

At this point, the amount left over should be huge because it includes the amount you used to pay on your mortgage and debts. You can increase monthly free-will offering in thanks to the LORD for helping you, to a much greater degree, reach the goals of *(1)* total debt freedom, *(2)* funding the spread of the gospel, *(3)* helping those in need, and *(4)* building wealth to maintain these priorities and take good care of yourself and family. Even after giving abundantly you will have much more to regularly invest than in the past. Also, you will be able to spend more than in the past. Each of these will be planned within your monthly budget so you are careful to not be yoked to the chains of debt bondage ever again. You will find your savings and investments growing so large that you will at times be able to spontaneously give huge sums of money from your treasuries to worthwhile endeavors within and outside of Church ministry.

Giving honors Him and opens the door for Him to mightily rebuke the devourer on your behalf and pour out blessings. Therefore, we know He is pleased by sacrificing and exercising self-control and rewards it to allow you even more money to spread the gospel and make disciples. Even though His authorities *(Church leaders)* receive your tithes and offerings on earth, Jesus Christ, who lives forevermore, receives them in Heaven. Not only will you receive an abundant supply for having sown in good ground, other people will be also able to glean great benefits from your harvests.

Faithfully adhering to the Seven Steps will discipline you to help you to consistently live beneath your take home pay. The focus they require also help you live in accordance with the Eleven Principles. They have boundaries within which you should operate in order to maintain wisdom, prudence, safety, security, and positive forward momentum in your life and finances. The LORD provides us with everything we need to fulfill His purpose and plan for our lives via knowledge, understanding, and wisdom received from our intimate relationship with Him through the Holy Spirit, who is always in concert with bible instruction.

The parable of the talents and minas share a few lessons with us. First, the LORD expects us to invest a portion of the money He provides throughout our lives. Second, He wants a reasonable portion to be put into investments with high-growth potential that could increase them 30, 60, 100, or 1,000-fold. Third, if we do not put money in investments with high-growth possibilities, He expects we would at least put a reasonable portion of the money in financial institutions to create compound interest growth on top of the original principle. Fourth, during The Final Judgment He will call people to account of their stewardship of life and money.

Some people wonder if they must invest in stocks at all or any other specific type of investment *(bonds, real estate, etc.)*. The bible tells you blessings and rewards *(such above average growth)* accompany consistent trading. This equates to investing in equity-based products like viable businesses, stocks, income properties, and the like.

Over long periods of time *(10 years or more)* the broad stock, bond, and real estate markets have historically experienced much higher growth on average than during short-term cycles. However, there is no guarantee this will always happen in the future. People who have greater risk tolerance will be willing to take the increased risk of investing in these vehicles because history shows them to be far better at producing long-term growth than putting money in low interest savings accounts and the like. Usually they will not panic and sell the investments they previously purchased when the market periodically goes south. Most increase their investment over the long run because of the enormous gains they reasonably expect to receive after 5, 10, or 20 years of investing.

People who don't have the risk tolerance to sit still through up and down investment market swings generally do the opposite and thus lose money. They buy stocks, bonds, real estate, or other things at high prices *(due to euphoria when market valuations are going up)* and sell at lower prices *(due to fear when market valuations are going down)*. When one truly has greater risk tolerance, he/she would probably always invest a significant percentage of his/her portfolio on a dollar cost averaging basis over the long-term *(equal periodic investments)*. He/she would likely only reduce their portfolio portions when absolutely necessary. Getting older and not having as much time to recoup sizeable market losses may be one reason. Most people would probably always keep at least 50% of their investments in the stock market at all times. This can be done expediently via an array of no-load low-expense stock index mutual funds.

Nobody knows when a down market will occur or rebound - not even market-timers and day-traders! That's why a very high percentage of them usually lose more money than they make trying to time stock trades. Looking to invest only when we think the market will go up creates a situation where you will usually experience substantial losses that will never be recovered because you will most often buy at high prices and sell at lower prices. If at the current time you simply do not have the risk tolerance to withstand the ups and downs for the long haul then there is nothing wrong with continuing to invest in low risk guaranteed return, fixed income, low cost annuity, stable value, certificate of deposit like investments in your retirement plans and brokerage accounts. Just remember, your gains may not beat inflation over the long haul. However, when you otherwise follow the Seven Steps you will still far outdo the vast majority of your peers who do not budget, eliminate debt, and save / invest on a consistent basis.

Our example of becoming multi-millionaires in about 20 years on public servant income by putting approximately 75% of our investment money into no-load low-expense stock index mutual funds and the remaining 25% into bonds and fixed income investments give insight into the power of employing a simple long-term investing pattern. You should use sound tools to determine your risk tolerance to decide how much stock *(equity)* investment you are comfortable with. At older ages, many people want a lower percentage of investment money affected by day-to-day swings in the stock market. Unfortunately, many of the same people fall hook, line, and sinker for scam artists who tell them they can give them higher than average returns on their money very quickly. Your best path is to forego the scam artist pitches and simply stick with the stock, bond, and real estate markets that have been proven to historically provide very good long-term returns.

I know average wage earners who amassed hundreds of thousands of dollars by investing in certificates of deposits and fixed income investments over their 30-40 year working lives and who continue to invest that way in retirement and they're doing well. If they are not living like kings and queens in their senior years *(when we all need comfort the most)*, they're certainly living like princes and princesses. The most important biblical money management principles you can follow are living beneath your take home pay, tithing, eliminating debt to live debt-free as soon as possible, refusing to co-sign, and regularly saving 10% and increasingly greater amounts over the course of your working life so you can receive the exponential benefit of compound interest.

While we believe investing in stocks over the long haul will provide greater asset accumulation and greater opportunities for giving and comfort in your senior years, before you do so you should educate yourself about such investments and make sure that you feel comfortable investing via such products regardless of what we or anyone else might advise. Until you are educated and comfortable with the risk you would be taking, let your savings *(via guaranteed and fixed income products)* be your investments. Saving and investing is an example of a principle having reasonable parameters within which you should operate in order for you and your family to be blessed and rewarded throughout your time on earth.

Be as simple as you can in managing your finances, so you are not stressed out. This usually requires less than 3 hours per week. When investing, employ dollar cost averaging and don't worry about short-term fluctuations in the investment markets. Only invest in a more-risky manner once you show good stewardship by making it to Step 7, develop expertise in various forms of investing, ensure your family is well cared for, and understand the risk of loss associated with such investment.

Much of your financial plan, money management, and investing can be self-directed using the simple Seven Step plan discussed above, however if you must hire a financial advisor to help you, pick one that *(a)* is knowledgeable and trustworthy, *(b)* will not charge you sales charges for purchasing investments, *(c)* will not try to sell you mutual funds that charge 12b-1 fees, and *(d)* will not charge you management fees greater than one-half of one-percent per year. Even when using an advisor, it behooves you to research and learn about investments so you maintain authority and direction over your money and rule out any guidance the advisor gives that does not sit well with you.

You should be in a position to intelligently decide which of his/her recommendations to use. Make no rash, quick decisions knowing there will always be tomorrow, which allows you to spend a few days verifying the historical pattern / record of the recommended investments and determining if they are risk you are willing to take over the long-term because you believe they fit your tolerance and will be as profitable as they need to be to help meet your goals.

Some people think a financial roadmap consisting of an overall vision with short, medium, and long-term goals destroy dreams. In reality, it wisely facilitates the ability of dreams to come to pass and does so in a manner that helps you be a good steward, maintain the dream, and live in financial peace. Your first inclination should be to ask the LORD what He wants from your stewardship of His money and how He wants you to spend it on things beyond needs for yourself, your family, and the Church.

The LORD has rewarded many average wage earners who used the simple, wise approach described above thus enabling them to: *(a)* give much more for good works that help others, *(b)* spread the gospel to a greater degree, *(c)* live totally debt-free by eliminating all their non-mortgage debt in a few years, *(d)* build huge net worth in less than twenty years, and *(e)* not have to worry about the ups and downs the economy cyclically endures. His wise plan produces a unique prosperous place for each person who consistently uses biblical financial principles.

Be thankful for the current blessings He provides and be forever content at every stage of life while serving His interests, giving abundantly, and doing good works in your community. Ultimately, your obedience to His principles will produce an ability to live at a more expensive level if He so desires. In order to be safely and securely in His blessing, your roadmap should focus on first taking care of that which is necessary, then on reaching for that which is possible yet difficult, and then you will find that He will help you do and live the impossible.

In 2009 numerous people said they wanted to start flipping or rent real estate. They believed it was the right time to get into the game because housing values in most parts of the United States had been reduced up to 40% off their 2006 record high levels. They heard that others were doing this very thing and were able to get foreclosed homes at even lower prices. Some heard banks were selling many foreclosed houses for as little as one dollar. It was true some banks reduced prices to get out from under foreclosed houses that cost them a great deal of money to sit on because they would have to maintain the properties and pay taxes while trying to wait for many years for the market to come back up in speculation that they could then sell to someone at much higher prices. However, it was an exaggeration that they were basically giving away very sound houses for next to nothing.

Even with the much lower housing prices many people paid more than their income and assets could handle. They also often had to make tens of thousands of dollars in cosmetic improvements and sometimes more in structural repairs. They filled their lives up with loans and many raided the little bit they had in retirement accounts to get fixer-uppers. They lost lots of money and owed huge sums when they did not have enough money to make needed repairs and thus could not sell the homes or rent them. Many were not good landlords and could not keep trustworthy renters in the homes / apartments or demand enough rent even on fixed-up places to cover the mortgages on the properties. They also did not have enough income or assets to maintain the properties and pay mortgages for many months or years when they were unable to flip or rent them. They needed a huge amount of cash saved in order to make these deals work. Many who had no understanding of how such investment works and/or did not have the necessary skill fell into foreclosure and/or bankruptcy just like many of those from whom the houses were previously taken.

This story was told from the standpoint of flipping and rental real estate investments but also relates to other types of investment for which one needs to obtain a deeper knowledge base and understanding of operations and how to profit before investing in them. There are some people uniquely skilled with a calling to invest in flipping, income-property, or other ventures. However, there are also many people who are not skilled and called to flipping, being a landlord, investing in commodities and futures, etc. and should not engage them until such time as they sit down with gifted people who have been profitable in these areas and truly understand how to become profitable themselves.

In the meantime, they should work to become totally debt-free and save money well beyond their three to six-month emergency fund so in due time they can *(with wisdom)* wade into investments that are more difficult with a much higher potential for growth. They also should consistently be investing at least 10% of gross monthly income *(and make sure they get all 401k employer match money)* with the bulk of it in a diversified portfolio of total U.S. market no-load low-expense stock index mutual funds and a pinch of it in U.S. no-load low-expense bond index funds.

If you have seriously prayed about an investment or business venture and truly believe the LORD is directing you to make such an investment, by all means you should at some point do it. However, you should not do it on a spur of the moment, throwing all understanding and wisdom to the wind, hoping to get-rich-quick. Research methods and processes financially successful Christians use. This will help you determine:

1. The position you need to be in.
2. The business plan you need to *craft (product, customer base, surplus needed, etc.).*

3. The daily, weekly, monthly, yearly actions you need to take to engage and make the business profitable.

4. The months or years you are likely to have to wait before the business produces positive cash flow and becomes profitable for you.

5. How you plan to distribute and use profits in ways that give the LORD glory *(gospel evangelism and disciple-making, caring for family, charitable giving, helping others in need, spending on desires, etc.)*.

On this seventh step and always, you should utilize personal financial budgeting for the income you take from the business for family use. This is a working, giving, saving, spending plan that helps you put yourself in position to invest a substantial amount of money in your ventures when necessary. Any business you start or maintain also needs a separate ongoing budget that helps guide it and it needs monthly cash flow statements and periodic drafting of income statements and balance sheets, so you know the condition that it is in and can remedy any problems that stifle it or might lead to it being unprofitable or liquidated. If you're in really bad financial condition, it may take you a couple of years to save money necessary to invest or start a business but you'll be better prepared and better off in the long run having eliminated debt and saving adequate emergency funds and ensuring that surplus cash flow and assets are available to start and successfully run a business.

Proverbs 27:12 shows that a prudent man sees danger and sidesteps it but the simple-minded walk right into it and suffer. So, don't be hasty to be rich. Instead:

A. Believe you will prosper.

B. Research the venture through which you want to prosper.

C. Write a plan identifying your macro vision of the venture that details the methods you'll use

D. Take action to achieve the desired results, and

E. Have patience in reaching each step on the ladder knowing in due time you will achieve the prosperous future that awaits you.

It is a blessing and reward having made it to the Seventh Step, from which many more visions and dreams are able to come to fruition, be extremely profitable, and produce ongoing wealth for future generations. Engaging the Eleven Principles and Seven Step Plan will catapult your life spiritually and financially in a Christ-like trajectory. You will be able to give, save, invest, and spend like never before in ways that align with first and foremost seeking the LORD and His ways so you are not aimed at the love of money, worldly ways, and material things.

Following the Seven-Step Plan will help you get to the point in budgeting, debt-freedom, monthly surplus where you will have greater disposable income and assets you could use within reason to help your children pay educational expenses and pursue worthwhile entrepreneurial efforts that can brighten their future.

Good money managers organize their lives to know when bills are due, know how much they owe, and pay their bills on time. They also immediately record all checking account deposits and withdrawals and balance their checkbooks every month to ensure they are able to pay future bills and to ensure money is not erroneously or illegally taken from their accounts. Godly stewards listen to the LORD's voice to understand how He would have them give, save, and spend within the boundaries of scripture concerning the lifestyle and financial focus Christians should maintain throughout their lives.

You should not purchase any products or services using credit when you do not already have more than enough money to pay off the account immediately. If you don't have cash on hand right now to buy it, then you should forego the purchase and allow Him to supernaturally bring it to you free of charge *(if you really need it)* or in a way that will not lead to possible financial bondage if your income producing projections don't work out like you envisioned.

If you don't have a Church, you need to find a bible believing Church and allow the Holy Spirit to plant you in that local representation of Christ's body. When you forsake the regular assembly of believers you cannot be truly fulfilled and prosperous no matter how much money you make or assets you have.

Your God-given purpose is intertwined with fellowship and discipleship within a local expression of the body of Christ. Thus, interacting with leaders and members within your local Church and other believers, you are called to make ministry service *(evangelism and discipleship of others)* the priority in your life that guides every other endeavor you pursue *(career, friendships, recreation, education, business, etc.).*

Following the Seven-Step plan above, you'll begin to accumulate assets at an astounding rate. The power of compound growth over the next 10, 20, and 30 years will exponentially expand your investments. You will begin to live the biblical instruction, "be fruitful and multiply...and have dominion over the Earth!" The biblically-based financial principles you follow and the increased income and assets He entrusts to you will allow you take dominion in every area of life, such as properly caring for your family, continued, uninterrupted tithing to your local Church, funding missions in your community and around the world, funding ministries you are directly and physically involved in as well as helping the poor, widows, and oppressed.

This wealth building scenario will not likely happen for you if you are not committed to living out the LORD's plan for you to be debt-free. You must forsake the temptation to create monthly bills that add up to an amount that is greater than 50% of your gross income. Setting your spending bar at this level will save you more financial trouble than you can imagine and allow you to carry out your abundant giving and wealth building financial plan in an optimum manner.

We did not include college funding as an individual step because financial plans operate best when they are like airplane emergency landing instructions. Make sure you put on oxygen and safety equipment first before attempting to help your children put on theirs. Otherwise, you will harm then by being a poor financial steward, by not investing for growth that can meet your future retirement needs, and by helping them making bad college choices that encumber you all in massive debt.

Allow Him to bless you with products and services you need that you can't pay cash for right now. If He doesn't bless you with them, then you don't really need them. Continue to have patience in following His financial plan and you'll soon find you can get not only what you need but many desires because you delight yourself in Him spiritually and financially. When your life is balanced in this way, abundant blessings cannot help but be poured out on you in due time.

Please email me at rparlo@ameritech.net or call 517-393-5081 so I can forward a sample Net Worth Statement and Giving Saving Spending Plan *(budget)* you can use to eliminate financial bondage and powerfully build wealth.

CHAPTER 3

ORGANIZE RECORDS AND BALANCE CHECKBOOKS

You must diligently organize financial records, balance checkbooks, and review all accounts to ensure errors are corrected *(bank, credit card, investment accounts, etc.)* in order to have a healthy financial life. At all times, good financial stewards know exactly how much money they have at their disposal or they are able to quickly find out from account ledgers. People who don't organize and immediately record deposits and deduct withdrawals from account balances are usually in poor financial shape. They often write checks and take on debt payments for more than they can afford to spend.

Getting a current account balance from a teller or looking at your checking account online doesn't show how much you really have to spend because many checks are cashed days or weeks after they're written. The fact that $1,000 was payroll deducted into your account on Friday doesn't mean that $1,000 is available for you to spend on desires until your next paycheck. You cannot know what you truly have available to spend unless you know what's in your account after you subtract all checks written and withdrawals and record monthly bills that have yet to be paid during the pay period. Also, you need to make sure there is enough money in your account to also pay unexpected bills that will periodically arise. In addition, you need to make sure your account balance will allow you to have enough extra income each pay period to eliminate your debt within a couple of years or sooner if possible and thereafter to invest 10% or more in vehicles that will provide enough annual compound growth to build wealth.

It's almost impossible to build an emergency fund, eliminate debt, and increase wealth without organizing financial records, balancing checkbooks, and reviewing accounts for errors. These practices help you know the state of your flocks and herds at all times so you can properly budget income, appropriately spend, save emergency funds, eliminate debt, and invest.

If you do not follow an organized accountability plan, financial institutions will rake you over the coals with non-sufficient fund fees, late fees, overdraft fees, and other account charges. In addition, you are likely to find yourself deeply in debt, possibly facing repossession, foreclosure, and/or bankruptcy. Open your eyes right now to see you can undo financial bondage, build wealth, and fulfill your God-given purpose when you properly manage money including organizing financial records, balancing your checkbooks, and reviewing all accounts to ensure errors are corrected.

There are a number of ways you can organize records for purposes of making sure all financial data is in a few locations that can be quickly and easily accessed in order to know the data that should be used to periodically complete net worth statements and household budgets *(giving-saving-spending plan)*, and to find current and past financial account information when needed.

1. Gather all the creditor billing statements *(including utilities, etc.)* that you have laying in piles on your tables, in drawers, and on floors. Make sure you at least have all the latest billing statements from all your creditors. For recordkeeping ease, put all billing statements in one filing system. Copy each billing statement creditors send you electronically each month. You may have to contact creditors to get copies of each billing statement so you have them all.

2. On a table, arrange each billing statement by day of each month on which payment is due from the 1st thru the 31st. When the payment due date fluctuates each month simply use the day of the month that tends to be the earliest due date ever requested by the creditor. For example, if your electric utility payment is generally due anywhere from the 12th to the 17th, then use the 12th as the payment due date for recordkeeping and budgeting purposes.

3. Once arranged in the above order, put all the bills in a filing system with tabs at the top of each folder / divider that shows the above noted day-of-the-month order for arranging records. The tab at the top of each folder / divider should be labeled with its own date from the 1st thru the 31st as well as the name of one specific creditor's billing statements that will be placed in that folder or behind that divider tab. When more than one creditor's payment due date occurs on the same date then you should have that same number of folders / dividers with the same due date but different creditor names on them. For example, 1st-Home Mortgage, 1st-Car Note, and 1st-Cable subscription.

4. You only need days of the month recognized on folder / divider tabs when a payment is due on that date from at least one creditor. So, if the next date on which a payment is due is the 5th of each month, then your next folder / divider tab should be similar to 5th-MSUFCU Visa.

5. You should keep the billing statements for each creditor in January through December order during each billing year, so you know the last one received is always the one for which payment is due or payment has been made. Keep at least one year of consecutive billing statements and you can usually get rid of any billing statements older than one-year.

6. You should put a monthly recurring appointment reminder on your computer calendar or smart phone calendar that reminds you by email or text of each creditor's payment

due date at least seven days in advance of the payment each month to ensure you do not miss checking your budget and paying the bill on time.

7. When you get calendar email or text notification that a payment is due, immediately refer to the latest billing statement for that creditor in the filing system to either write a check and mail it, or use a phone payment option, or an online payment option.

This recordkeeping system provides organization you need to identify *(a)* the consistency of each month's payment due date for each creditor, *(b)* the amount due over the past year for each creditor, and *(c)* other data that will be helpful in charting your financial future via ongoing monthly budgets and periodic net worth statements. Without it or a similarly organized system you will make mistakes in payment timing and financial decision-making that will cost you dearly over the years by keeping you in financial bondage and outside of the wealth building process.

In this technology age, you do not usually need to physically store / maintain records produced by financial institutions *(including banks / credit unions, brokerages, mutual fund companies, and investment companies)* that hold assets and that are not creditors issuing monthly bills. This includes 401k statements, bank accounts, brokerage accounts, and similar statements. They allow easy online access to your account information so you are able to see the amount of your investments over the past few years including deposits and withdrawals.

Make sure you have safe user ID's and passwords to protect you from identity fraud and theft. Passwords with two-tier authentication and that contain some capital letters, symbols, lower case letters, numbers usually provide a good level of safety, but this can change over time so be careful to keep up on the latest safety info and periodically change account passwords for greater protection. Also, access your accounts at least once each month to *(a)* ensure data does not appear to be breached, *(b)* review accounts for data entry errors, *(c)* know if you need to inform your financial institutions to correct any errors, and *(d)* balance *(reconcile)* your checkbooks and other accounts based on deposits, withdrawals, account fees, etc.

In a safe accessible location for you but hidden from everyone else except your spouse, those to whom you given durable power of attorney for finances, and/or those you've appointed as executors of your will, keep a record of all your financial institutions websites and account access information *(ID's, passwords, and security question answers)*. This provides reasonably prompt access to your financial accounts anytime you want to review information or make changes or they need to access accounts when you are incapacitated or deceased in order to handle your or your estates business.

WARNING! WARNING!

Tossing your mail / bills in the corner and refusing to open them each month, like some people have done in the past, will not take you to the financial promise land. You will dwell in a dry, poverty-stricken desert or fail to reach your full financial potential & ministry calling. You will not dwell in The Wealthy Place the LORD desires for you to be blessed and a blessing to many others.

If you are to really know the state of your flocks and herds per Proverbs 27:23 so you can count the cost per Luke 14:28 to ascertain whether or not your monthly budget can cover the purchase of desired merchandise and services, then you must weekly consult and regularly update data in your financial records filing system. After the day or so it takes to set up an appropriate recordkeeping system, it will only take a couple of hours per week to review, maintain, and use it to make appropriate bill payments and measure financial wherewithal.

Organizing your records allows you to put the Eleven Principles into action. Monthly balancing your checkbook against your checking account and regularly reviewing all financial institution accounts is necessary to ensure errors are corrected and data is accurate. This helps you truly know the discretionary income and assets at your disposal to maximize the Seven Step plan by shortening the time it takes for you to get out of financial bondage and into The Wealthy Place.

A worksheet with instructions for balancing your checkbook against your checking account is readily available from your bank or credit union and easy to follow when performed monthly on a step-by-step basis. Some institutions call them account reconciliation forms. Make sure you have online access to bank / credit union account statements. If not, keep at least one-year of paper statements in a file. Those for different banks should be kept in their own folder by year and month issued, from January thru December.

If you have never balanced your checkbook against your checking account or have not balanced them in a long time, you should make an appointment with a bank / credit union representative to have them go over the balancing method so you know exactly where your funds stand. You will need the accurate account balance *(that accounts for all checks and other obligations written on the account that have not yet been paid)* to ensure an accurate account of your balance each month going forward. This helps you maintain control of your account so money is not leaking out of it and you can be propelled forward into greater giving, saving/investing, and wealth building.

Failing to regularly balance checkbooks against checking accounts keeps many people in a continual pattern of paying insufficient funds fees and other charges because bad financial habits and mishaps remain uncorrected. In most instances, if you wait too long to report a mishap you may never be able to get it corrected in your favor. You will lose the withdrawals that you failed to catch in a timely manner. You should want to make sure all money that is supposed to be deposited in your account is actually deposited into your account and that no money is withdrawn from your account except that which you acknowledge / confirm should be withdrawn.

When you get the budget process rolling along, your ongoing

budget should mimic your checkbook ledger. When you are immediately recording deposits and withdrawals *(including checks written)* and consistently paying bills when due, you are on a path to alleviating financial bondage by correcting past irresponsible financial behavior. Over the next year or so, your credit history and score will get much better and even more so as you press forward to pay more than the minimum due on monthly bills and to totally eliminate debt from your financial portfolio.

CHAPTER 4

JOB SEARCH AND ENTREPRENEURIAL ENDEAVORS

Years ago, I felt unsatisfied and unfulfilled in a hum drum, monotonous life until a burst of light entered my heart to let me know I would never understand the purpose and calling for which I was created without putting my faith in the grace of Jesus Christ to save me and set me free from the futility of my own desires and those expressed by people around me.

The LORD taught me how and when to write goals related to pursuing *(1)* deeper intimacy with Him and His Church, *(2)* sharing biblical truth and the testimony of what He is doing in my life with other people (evangelism), and *(3)* helping lead other people to Him so they have an opportunity to be disciples also.

These three principles are the guiding priority for my communication and actions for my life, work, and service to others. I ask Him to help me faithfully make widgets, provide worthwhile service, initiate & complete projects, and help others in a way that gives Him the glory and allows me to live in the abundance of righteousness, peace, joy, money, and resources He desires for my life.

His methods for using me *(in employment and entrepreneurial endeavors)* change from time to time, however these three principles remain the focal point from which everything flows. As a believer, I

126

look forward with purpose to the things I am working on and doing while on Earth and to spending eternity with Him in Heaven and the New Earth after my days here are done.

Peruse the following websites *(and similar ones in your locale)* to find permanent and temp opportunities you can apply for in order to gain employment. As much as possible, you should get names and phone numbers of human resources managers for the businesses / organizations and call, communicate, or visit them weekly to keep their minds thinking about you so they know you are a person with perseverance who will not give up until they give you a job opportunity.

If necessary, to get your foot in the door, approach businesses *(with whom long-term employment is desirable)* with the fact that you are willing to do an unpaid internship for a short time to show you're dependable and talented and can add great value to their bottom-line. In addition, you may also want to contact Salvation Army, Red Cross, Volunteers of America, Rescue Missions, Good Will Industries, AARP, and other non-profits about job openings and volunteer opportunities that could turn into a permanent job.

http://www.mitalent.org

https://www.governmentjobs.com/careers/michigan

https://hr.msu.edu/aro/Applicants.html

http://lansingmi.gov/1221/Employment-Opportunities

https://www.indeed.com/l-Lansing,-MI-jobs.html

http://ardjc.tripod.com/jvdfz/jobs-lansing-mi-area.html

https://www.monster.com/

https://www.taskrabbit.com/become-a-tasker

https://www.freelancer.com/

https://support.freelance.com

https://www.moonlighting.com/

https://www.upwork.com/?

https://www.flexingit.com/

https://www.yelp.com/search?find_loc=Lansing,+MI&start=20&cflt=employmentagencies

http://jobs.usatoday.com/Register/Step1/utm_source=marketing&utm_medium=email&utm_campaign=GannettJS&utm_content=USAToday

https://jobs.aarp.org/v#index.php%3Fpage%3Dsearch%26action%3Dadvanced_search%26keywords%3Dpart%2Btime%26CMP%3DEMC-MIM-DIS-OTH-WORKJOBS-CONSUMER2018-TGT-20180530_WorkJobs_Part-TimeWork_Initial_325400_593401-20180530-Hero-Hero_Image-Image-PRT-2984140%26encparam%3DkmDE1VuKmYlVSOqyqxZiqXsGboUNnXIecsTYJzrdxvU%253D

Below is guidance for beginning an entrepreneurial endeavor that can help you produce income and gain valuable work experience as you move forward. I call this the initial Who, What, When, Where, Why Plan.

1. *An entrepreneurial endeavor need only start with a list of types of work you can do to produce extra revenue and make a profit.*

For example: cleaning people's homes, babysitting, window cleaning, consulting based on expertise, lawn mowing, snow shoveling, hedge trimming, gutter cleaning, bookkeeping, etc.

This will enable you to tithe and give more, build suitable emergency funds for the inevitable rainy day, eliminate debt, provide more options & better comfort for your family, and fund other important endeavors.

2. *Choose one of the types of work to pursue.*

For purposes of the following parts of an initial business plan I will use cleaning people's homes as the example entrepreneurial venture.

3. *Describe how you would do it and how much it will cost to get started.*

For example: I will use cleaning products I already have or my clients already have to do room cleaning for other people and as soon as I get paid by one or more of them I will *(a)* set aside 25% of net revenue in a separate business account to pay federal state, and city income and other taxes and fees, *(b)* put at least 10% of net revenue in an emergency reserve account, *(c)* use 25% of net revenue to pay business expenses & debt, *(d)* use no more than 25% of net revenue to replenish products and tools for future cleaning jobs, and *(e)* use some of it to pay off business debt and pay myself the remainder and put it toward paying off personal debt. I will use products I already have, therefore *(if this is not a business that was started some time age and now has debts)* it will not cost anything to start except $20 for flyers or business cards. I believe it would cost $50 to start if I had to buy cleaning products.

4. *Identify the market of people or businesses you will approach to get paid work of the type you are pursuing.*

For example: I will approach every home or rental unit occupant within a four-block radius in my neighborhood. I will make flyers or business cards to hand out and put on billboards. I will craft a 30-second introduction I can share with homeowners and renters to help them understand the great service I will provide to make their lives better.

5. *Identify when you will initiate action to pitch your work to people, how often each week and how many you will approach, along with a schedule that lists the dates and times you can perform the work for paying customers.*

For example: I will start pitching my product and service next Monday. I will approach at least four new homeowners each Monday, Tuesday, and Thursday from 6pm to 8pm. I will declare I am not afraid of rejection because it is normal for the majority of pitches to be rejected and that overtime a few clients here and there will build into many to help me be profitable in my endeavor.

A fully developed business plan is not often necessary for starting no cost / low cost entrepreneurial activities designed to make hundreds to thousands of dollars monthly to help you quickly increase income for debt elimination, saving, and investing purposes. For example, the following types of endeavors and many others fit the bill - home cleaning, tutoring, baking, dance lessons, music lessons, creating websites for small businesses, providing computer hardware / software services, physical fitness trainer, business consulting using expertise *(knowledge, ability, skill, etc.).*

Often, such endeavors only need *(a)* physical / mental effort to gain clients, *(b)* simple paper flyers or business cards describing what you offer, *(c)* social media marketing among your friendships that asks them to refer others who can use your product / service, *(d)* scheduled time and resolve to pick neighborhoods or other venues to knock on doors and approach people to introduce your product

/ service, and *(e)* great resolve to not stop even if the bulk of people approached do not respond or tell you "no."

If each product/service gains you $50 after expenses and only 2 of 10 people approached each week purchase it, then you would make $400 in one month with an ability to increase your revenue and profit in future months as you pick up sales steam via *(1)* rave reviews from customers about how it meets their need or desire, *(2)* new customers and repeat purchasers, *(3)* customer referrals to friends, *(4)* reasonably increased time and effort put towards gaining additional sales, and *(5)* better administrative efficiencies concerning scheduling sales and service, providing customer service excellence, and limiting monthly expenses to purchases that are well below product/service revenue and that are absolutely necessary and best for serving your customers with excellence.

Below are a few tools that may help your entrepreneurial endeavor be more profitable or help you eventually turn it into a full-fledged business:

1. The book EntreLeadership by Dave Ramsey (debt-free business creation and management) at www.Amazon.com and visit the website https://www.entreleadership.com/.
2. Business Boutique at www.businessboutique.com/.
3. Make an appointment for free business plan consulting with the LCC Small Business Development Center 483-1921 or an SBDC at a community college or university near you. When the counselor brings up business financing, let him/her know you plan to start and maintain your business on a cash flow basis without obtaining loans, loan payments, any type of debt, or lease obligations you do not currently have assets to cover in full throughout the lease term.
4. A business plan is often a key element to starting successful entrepreneurial endeavors, especially business building activities. You may not have initially started out by designing a business plan, but you will likely need one eventually. So,

it is best you take time now to develop one as a roadmap to help your entrepreneurial endeavor succeed and along the way tweak it as necessary to help you grow and bring a great return on your time, money, and emotional capital to be invested in the endeavor you choose. Some elements you may need in your plan:

a. Executive Summary – this succinctly describes your business, the seasons in which it plans to operate, and how you plan to grow your business. Also, estimate the number of months or years it will take to make the business profitable.

b. A Mission Statement – what your company is in business to do.

c. Description of your products and services and prices you will charge for each one.

d. Describe what sets your business apart from others via the need you are filling and things you offer that your competitors do not.

e. The market of people, businesses, and organizations you will approach to buy your products and services and your method of product and service delivery.

f. Description of business structure including an organization chart that includes employee position titles and brief description of duties. Also, describe work for which you expect to use independent contractors?

g. Financial information.

4.g.i. Monthly building rent / mortgage payment, equipment purchases, staff salaries, etc. you anticipate to start, maintain, and grow the business.

4.g.ii. Source and amount of assets and cash flow you will use to pay for monthly business expenses when business revenues are not adequate to pay.

4.g.iii. The anticipated monthly revenue stream and net profit you expect to generate selling products and services or soliciting donations.

4.g.iv. Estimated annual business budget, fiscal year income statement, and balance sheet.

h. Summary of your future plans for the business, like timing of expanded product lines, new or enhanced services, etc.

5. AARP provides tips and tools at <u>Entrepreneurship</u> to help you along your journey of becoming an entrepreneur or starting a business. The Small Business Administration also has a business plan tool at <u>www.sba.gov/business-guide/plan-your-business/write-your-business-plan</u>, that gives you step-by-step guidance. A business plan can help you determine whether a business endeavor *(a)* is a good fit for your life and the economic / financial environment you are in, and *(b)* is likely to be profitable within a reasonable amount of time or is a waste of time, money, and emotional capital on an unprofitable idea. It helps you ditch unprofitable ideas and move forward to measure the viability of the next entrepreneurial endeavor you envision.

6. The Sunday edition of most local newspapers usually have a page that shows you where business plan workshops will be held within the next week or two. They can be good sources to engage to help you craft a business plan.

The following resources may also be helpful. Normally, for any type of funding to be provided by such sources you will need to be at the stage where you have developed a business plan and brief business pitch. The people who hear / view your pitch will have to believe your idea or current endeavor will likely be reasonably profitable over time. The information and help provided by the resources above and below can help you get into that position. You will need to find similar resources in your community to help you along this journey.

Michigan Business Incubators
Can help you grow and find venture capital firms that might invest in you
http://www.michipreneur.com/michigan-business-incubators-and-workspaces/

Transformation Gems
transformationgems@gmail.com
1-805-994-0822
https://transformationgems.com/

Start Garden
40 Pearl St NW #200, Grand Rapids, MI 49503
https://g.co/kgs/6Jvy4H

Top Ten Crowdfunding Websites for businesses
https://www.entrepreneur.com/article/228534

Top 10 Crowdfunding Websites for Nonprofits
http://www.crowdcrux.com/top-10-crowdfunding-sites-for-nonprofits/

Below is helpful guidance regarding Reference and Interview Expectations when you need to hire staff. Sometimes, it is difficult to know what managers are looking for in a new hire, so I will give you things I generally look for in a candidate.

1. The person understands the purpose of the business and job he / she is interviewing for and in general what the daily duties and tasks would be.

2. The person is able to show that past experience, training, and/or education correlates to the type of responsibilities and duties he / she would handle in the new-hire position.

3. The person can describe current skills and past experience in a way that helps the interviewers believe he / she could handle the duties and responsibilities of the new-hire position.

4. The person has an aptitude and skill to be able to utilize the types of technological tools that must be used to perform the job, record results, and help the work unit evolve into a more efficient workplace as we move into the future.

5. The person understands that there is always more to know and understand about the work and will seek to learn through appropriate conversations with co-workers, stakeholders, classes, and research *(internet, libraries, conversations with experts in the field, etc.).*

6. The person's personality, demeanor, work-relationships, interpersonal skills, and dress patterns fit agency standards and would fit well with the current work unit staff members.

7. The person is an out-of-the-box thinker who is able to follow business / work unit standards yet also identify better ways of doing work and to increase customer service and profitability.

8. The person identifies problem areas and identifies solutions.

9. The person is able to brainstorm and collaborate with the supervisor and other staff to implement problem solutions and best practices.

10. The person's current and past supervisors would vouch for his / her ability to excel at the work assigned and also that he / she showed:

a. Initiative for completing assigned work.

b. Openness to taking on new assignments that may require development of new skills, being the kind of person who in down times *(low workload in various periods)* would get to know the entire work unit responsibilities well enough that he / she would not usually need to ask the supervisor to assign more work or a project, rather he / she would use knowledge of the work unit and conversations with other staff members to help identify, plan, and do projects that will help him / her, the work unit, and/or other staff members do their jobs better.

c. Ability to learn new things quickly.

d. Good decision-making ability, knowing when he / she generally has the flexibility to engage a different way of doing work versus the need to get the approval from the supervisor to engage a different way.

e. Creativity in using technological tools to help perform and complete her work and best display results for supervisor, management, and for performance measurement reports. This includes thinking about new ways work could be better performed, customers could be better served, and available technological tools can be better utilized.

Responses that speak to these criteria can be interwoven in responses to the various interview questions and would be things that references from current and former supervisors could vouch for. One who is interviewing for a position should, prior to the interview, call the manager of the work unit that is going to interview you and ask if there is more specific information about the work unit and work responsibilities that can be shared that might not generally be known. Also, ask questions about anything you do not understand concerning the work unit, its responsibilities, and duties of the position for which you are interviewing. New knowledge and understanding can then be weaved into interview responses for the entire panel of interviewers. Also, develop a couple of thoughtful questions to ask at the end of each interview. Communicate that you would exceed performance expectations if selected because have a grasp of the work unit responsibilities and position duties. Finally, communicate that your past experience, potential, and ability to work effectively with others are ideal for the position.

As you know, the bottom line for a Christian interviewee *(more than anything)* is seeking the Holy Spirit's guidance and following every instruction He gives while asking Him to help you display no fear or nervousness while in the interview. After you've done all you can, you just stand, and the LORD will ultimately move authority figures to place you in positions meant for you to get where His blessing is laid up for you and your service can be faithfully provided as a blessing to others. Sometimes in His desire to bless you to be a blessing in the marketplace mission field He wants you, He will move you into a position that is far beyond where your experience and schooling, etc. have been aimed by moving on the employer's heart to bypass lack of experience in areas where it is not truly needed.

CHAPTER 5

CAREER AND COLLEGE INFORMATION

Here is helpful information including scholarship website links below that may help you find enough scholarships to help your sons/daughters attend training or college on a debt-free basis or low-cost basis.

1. First and foremost, consistently and continually pray and invite the LORD to direct your paths and open doors that fit the LORD's marketplace and ministry plan for your son/daughter's life and to close doors that are not right for them and to help him/her attend school debt-free, so he/she will have maximum flexibility when choosing which career path to follow.

2. Write down the vision you believe the LORD has concerning your son/daughter's schooling, career, and ministry path *(i.e., to get training to obtain a certificate in media technology; an associate's in gaming; a bachelor's in gaming; a job creating games; etc.)* including specific things you will do to help fulfill that vision *save money to help pay a quarter of college / training expenses, help make contact with scholarship and grant organizations, etc.).* Also, have your son/daughter write

his/her vision and plan, compare yours with his/hers, and complete research with them to help him/her understand the best path and the resources available to them *(scholarships, internships, money, etc.)*. Explain the biblically-based need for each of you to pursuing the vision and plan on a debt-free basis.

3. Have your son/daughter attend a high school in your area that provides an early college program that pays for him/her to take community college credits that allow him/her to earn an associate degree along with a diploma upon graduation from high school. This will save tens of thousands of dollars on higher ed costs and put your son/daughter several years ahead of their peers toward earning a bachelor's degree and successfully entering the workforce and a career path. Also, by the time your son/daughter is a freshman in high school, start using the scholarship search websites at the bottom of this chapter to research grants, scholarships, and stipends they can qualify for along with the grade point average and community volunteer / work history, etc. they must have to get them. Finally, call all local associations *(chamber of commerce, retailers association, community organizations, etc.)* as well as numerous businesses to ask where you can submit a letter / application requesting grant, scholarship, and stipend consideration for your son or daughter who will be pursuing college or vocational training. It is never too late to research these sources for young adults who are already in college or training.

4. Also, research local scholarship programs *(Lansing Hope, Kalamazoo Promise, etc.)* that pay full tuition at a local community college for the first two years to obtain an associate degree, so the only thing your son/daughter must get scholarships and grants for is the additional two years to get a bachelor's degree debt-free.

5. Within the next month, you and your son/daughter should speak with a few professors at training schools and colleges who teach the curriculum of interest. Share your vision & goals and ask them for information on the median salary for desired positions within desired industries to which the education / training applies. Find out the true cost of the tuition and the starting salary & benefits and the salary progression for applicable jobs in the industries so you all understand whether training or a degree aimed at that industry is truly worthwhile.

6. Ask the professors to identify five businesses in your metro area that utilize people with the specific training your son/daughter is considering pursuing, so he/she can approach the business' human resources departments about paid or unpaid internships or shadowing one of their employees in each of their departments for a few weeks to see how they perform their duties, to engage innovative/creative ideas, and to provide value to the business while interning with them.

7. Ask the professors and business managers how they can help your son/daughter touch base with people in the desired industries that may pay for training or college and help your son/daughter get a good paying job upon completing training or degrees.

8. Encourage your son/daughter to continue to communicate with the professors and business managers throughout their training, so the plan can be tweaked along the way when necessary for maximum benefit for career and ministry.

9. Do not be put off by (a) a refusal of any professor or business to talk with you or (b) negative talking fear-filled professors / advisors. Just move on to the next professor, advisor, or business person until you get at least a couple that want to provide insight and/or resources that can help you succeed on the selected career path.

10. Any experience your son/daughter can get will help him/her get a foot in the door and put him/her far ahead of peers when it comes time to pursue employment or establish his/her own entrepreneurial / consulting endeavor.

11. Maintain this pattern of communication with professors and business people and the pattern of seeking internships, so you are highly sought after once you are ready for full-time work.

12. Start researching info about your training and career field via the internet and start talking to community college and university financial aid offices so they can also identify costs for training certificates and degrees and identify scholarships and grants for people pursuing the fields in which you or your kids are interested. The goal is to get enough scholarships and grants to be able to go to school debt free.

13. Encourage your son/daughter when he/she is in training school or college to connect with at least a few of the brightest students so they all can sharpen one another, help each other complete the training or degree, and ready each other to begin their careers in the industry.

14. Encourage your son/daughter to engage scientific, artistic, community-based endeavors in high school and college because such endeavors in his/her portfolio will give him/her an advantage over most candidates seeking jobs in the desired industry. Also, it will be of great help if they decide pursuing an entrepreneurial endeavor and equity investment is best for his/her long-term future.

Continue to PRAY with and for your kids daily, weekly, etc. while they are growing up, for the LORD to show them and you the work He made them to do and the steps necessary to get them there and allow them to infuse evangelism and disciple-making of others into the education process and as they engage in the work-a-day world up to and after college or vocational school or skilled trades apprenticeship, etc. Some kids are simply not made for college, so don't try to fit a square peg in a round hole.

Teach and encourage them to pursue good grades through hard work and study. 3.0 GPA and above normally gets the best college opportunities and scholarships. Start researching and having them take ACT and SAT tests during 9th grade thru 12th grade. Search out the local and state tuition promise programs as they may offer your kids free money for school. Consider low cost community college first and technical schools or skilled trades apprenticeships instead as well as public colleges instead of private colleges unless the latter will give you tuition, room, and board discounts that make them cost less than public colleges and low enough for you and your parents to pay without incurring debt.

Student loans are ridiculous in the huge burden they put upon young people and their families. Currently, they average approximately $35,000 for a bachelor's degree and costs much more at some colleges. People who take out the loans act ridiculously in terms of the amount borrowed and unnecessary things they spend the money on. Roughly 38% of student loan money is spent on student lifestyle *(designer clothes, partying, drinking alcoholic beverages, toys, computer games, etc.)*. While in college the student should work at least 20 hours per week and hopefully tie it into something related to his / her major by his/her sophomore year.

Look into college work study programs / jobs as well as other on and off campus income-earning options. This will help reduce the cost of school. Also, it will produce some income for the student to be able to help care for needs, do some desirable things while in school, and save money to prepare for rent down payments and other post college costs as they enter the grown-up work-a-day world. This process is necessary for them to be able to put on their big boy and big girl pants.

Remember, most schools cannot guarantee your son/daughter a job after graduation and they do not know if your son/daughter will secure work that provides median wages or greater. In addition, most customers / clients do not ask doctors and lawyers which schools their degrees are from. They might ask friends about good and bad experiences with doctors and lawyers, when they need to use one, and might make sure they are properly licensed by their state government. Most people do not even do the latter. Likewise, the majority of employers will not care where your training or degree(s) are from as long as the training institutions / colleges are appropriately accredited. Also, they will generally have positive feelings concerning entrepreneurial efforts. They will be greatly interested in how good your son/daughter is at their craft and that it benefits the business to utilize their education, skills, and potential. So, DO NOT over-spend for training or any educational degree. Again, do a cost / benefit analysis to make sure the pay and benefits the employment *(type of work)* will allow your son/daughter to obtain will be far greater *(in three to five years)* than the amount that would have to be paid to complete the training / education.

http://www.crosswalk.com/family/career/how-to-explore-careers-after-graduation.html

Below are scholarship websites to help begin your research.

www.Collegedebtsentence.com

MALDEF

Welcome to Hispanic Scholarship Fund | HSF

Faith and Education

http://www.thebestschools.org/blog/2012/12/10/20-colleges-providing-free-tuition/

discusawards.com

zinch.com

fastweb.com

scholarshippoints.com

cappex.com

www.thebestschools.org/blog/2012/1

https://www.myscholly.com/

https://bigfuture.collegeboard.org/pay-for-college

https://bigfuture.collegeboard.org/pay-for-college/grants-and-scholarships/where-to-find-college-scholarships

http://mycollegeguide.org/blog/04/2010/colleges-income-students-free-tuition-loans-full-rides/

http://www.finaid.org/questions/noloansforlowincome.phtml

http://www.collegedata.com/cs/search/scholar/schola

www.scholarshipinformer.com

How to win the search for college scholarships

https://www.commonapp.org/

https://commonblackcollegeapp.com/

CHAPTER 6

INSURANCE AND ESTATE PLANNING

A couple of other issues you need to be cognizant of, if you have not already taken care of them, are term life insurance and estate / healthcare planning.

It is wise to provide for each spouse's and each dependent's needs if a spouse predeceases the other one. To calculate the minimum life insurance need, one must consider separately *(1)* each spouse's annual income, *(2)* the amount of debt the household has *(house notes, car notes, Art Van furniture notes, Kay Jewelers notes, etc.)* that the other spouse will have to pay, *(3)* the annual cost of any other services that the deceased spouse provides or that his/her income currently pays for, and *(4)* the age of the youngest dependent. This data then helps you determine the life insurance policy amount that the widowed spouse needs in order to draw from to pay off all the debt represented by number *2* above and to draw a monthly income to take care of the things the deceased spouse formerly took care of per number 3 above.

For example, if the *(1)* wife's current annual income is $58,000 and the husband's current annual income is $42,000, and *(2)* total household debt is $150,000, *(3)* the annual cost of the deceased spouse's former services that the widowed husband must replace is $25,000 annually *(for childcare, housecleaning, portion of income covering autistic child therapy, etc.)* and the amount the widowed wife must replace is $15,000 *(for childcare, yard maintenance, minor home repairs, portion of income covering child's medical treatments)*, and *(4)* the age of the youngest dependent is 5, then the minimum amount of term life insurance the wife needs the husband to have is $375,000 and the minimum amount the husband needs the wife to have is $525,000.

That would allow the widow to pay off all the debt, invest the remainder of the money in a conservative mix of total stock market index and total intermediate bond index mutual funds, and withdraw a reasonable monthly income *(about 5% annually of the investment amount)* to complement his/her current earned income. Another way some advisors look at it is to have a policy limit that is at least 10 times your annual gross income because on average this would tend to cover the total payoff of remaining debt and allow for a withdrawal of money each month for the next 15 to 20 years to cover needed services the deceased spouse no longer provides. The husband's policy would then be at least $420,000 and the wife's policy would then be $580,000.

This could be obtained through a combination of employer supplied life insurance coverage as well as shopping for quotes from independent life insurance companies. Term insurance is the most straight-forward type and is pure security without a savings component imbedded in it, thus it tends to be 10 to 20 times cheaper than other forms of whole life / cash value life insurance policies. Diligent people committed to becoming and staying debt free and building wealth will do better buying term life insurance and saving and investing the way I note throughout this book, rather than purchasing whole life / cash value life insurance policies. They will generally have more money upon the death of a spouse.

The best financial plan is to work to become debt-free and outgrow your need for life insurance by having adequate assets to draw from in case of emergency and during retirement. Thus, you would buy a 20 to 30-year term policy that is a guaranteed renewal for the same annual price for the duration of the policy. After this time frame, your assets should be so vast *(likely in the millions)* that you have no need for life insurance coverage because you can more than handle any situation that arises. The spouse should always be the primary policy beneficiary and the children should be secondary beneficiaries.

Also, you need a *(a)* Will, *(b)* Durable Power of Attorney for Health Care (Patient Advocate Form), and *(c)* Durable Power of Attorney for Finances so your wishes upon death are spelled out and your assets flow correctly to the proper people *(spouse, kids, guardians)* and so upon incapacity *(coma, etc.)* or ill health your financial and health care representative*(s)* can make financial and health care choices in line with your wishes. It is likely your primary beneficiary and representative for the will and the other documents would be your spouse but you should also name a secondary beneficiary and representatives in case something were to also happen to your spouse at that time that would render him / her unable to fulfill the duties outlined by these documents.

You should seek the advice of a competent attorney if you do not feel comfortable that your state's statutory Will, Patient Advocate Form, and Durable Financial Power of Attorney documents meet your needs. Pertinent forms for simple estates can be found at the links below or a similar links related to your state of residence.

http://www.legislature.mi.gov/documents/publications/peaceofmind.pdf *(pages 25 and 35)*

http://www.michigan.gov/documents/reinventretirement/Financial_Toolkit_469363_7.pdf *(page 69)*

If the do-it-yourself estate planning documents do not meet your needs, you should call a few attorneys to see if their prices are acceptable for preparation of these documents. Compare their services and cost so you can choose the best one for you.

You may also want to ask them about the benefits of a Ladybird Deed and whether or not your state allows the passing on of property in this manner to beneficiaries *(children or other people)* so it does not have to go through the probate process upon the death of the current owner. He or she retains full ownership and right of conveyance while he / she lives, but immediately upon death the property is passed to the beneficiary who only need file a death certificate with the jurisdictional Register of Deeds. It works like the beneficiary / payable-on-death *(POD)* options available on 401k, brokerage, bank, and similar saving / investment accounts.

CONCLUSION

Due to a recessionary economy or bear market that usually occurs once every ten years or so, but only lasts an average of eighteen months, it seems many people suffer great personal financial and business loss and many experience car repossession, property foreclosure, and/or bankruptcy. These recessions bring high unemployment and loss of income, where all of a sudden, they have more in monthly debt payments than their monthly income can handle. Unfortunately, many people do not have much in the way of investments and have a heavy concentration of those assets in one company or one sector of the market and usually in a faddish one whose value fell precipitously when the recession reared its head. They simply have not put much away for the future, which has now come. All of sudden investments they thought would protect them are not enough to cover the debt payments they owe. Do you realize that having $100,000 or $200,000 or $300,000 in investments only allows you to draw about $$5,000 or $10,000 or $15,000 annually? Monthly this translates to $416 or $833 or $1,249. This is a pittance compared to the current median annual household income of approximately $60,000. It is anywhere from 8% to 24% of what a family needs to retain the lifestyle it is currently living.

Poor stewardship practices that result in people experiencing a downward financial spiral are failure to:

- Pursue other income earning opportunities via second jobs and no cost, low cost entrepreneurial endeavors.
- Refuse to use debt.
- Establish a budget to intimately know income and appropriately manage expenses.
- Eliminate debt during past rising economies and bull markets when they had increased revenue and income.
- Quickly reduce unnecessary expenses when they see signs of economic trouble.
- Build an emergency fund in high yield savings accounts at banks or credit unions in order to be able to continue to pay their expenses in emergency situations *(firings, layoffs, disability, etc.)*.
- Put at least 10% of gross monthly income in no-load low-expense total stock market index mutual funds with a conservative amount of that in no-load, low-expense intermediate bond index mutual funds that have a long-term history of excellent annual growth.
- Diversify assets by putting portions in different classes of investment with seven or eight brokerage houses *(Vanguard, Fidelity, TIAA-CREF, TD Ameritrade, etc.)*.
- Understand that taking on more debt will NOT help them alleviate financial problems.

Increasing your financial education via the right sources will help you understand that taking on more debt does not lead to debt elimination rather it leads to debt accumulation. It also helps you find equity investments that have a history of solid long-term growth so you can choose them for your diversified portfolio and control emotions to maintain your investments when there are short-term market gyrations. Most people do not reap huge long-term growth because they constantly buy investments at high prices and sell them at low prices due to emotions getting the better of them when markets go down or recessions come. In addition, good financial education will help you avoid speculative investments and business deals that would become worthless before you could sell them or get your money back.

Even the most astute investors will experience short-term losses in equity markets. However, they quickly subside *(in an average of 18 months)* and the market roars back to a point much higher than it was before it went down. In addition, recessionary economies and bear markets do not negatively affect every business and type of investment. There are always some that thrive when others experience losses. Thus, you have the ability to overcome losses and experience tremendous growth when you engage the biblically based discipline of good stewardship and diversification of investment assets.

Many people think abundant living is something reached once you amass a million dollars or more in assets because this is often the financial status people focus on as the one where a person becomes rich. Not to mention, people often give even greater accolades to those that earn million-dollar incomes. Almost every voice around us, even some in the Church, lift up people in these two categories as icons of the LORD's will for each man.

Certainly, being a millionaire is a great positions to be in, as long as the path that leads one there is directly in line with the personal calling the LORD made you for, a lifestyle that pleases Him and leads other people to Him, and a plan in the center of His will to serve other people good products and services. Many occupations please Him and some do not *(like pornography, filthy art forms, and crime)*. There are many character traits pleasing to Him yet some that are not pleasing *(like arrogance, lying, deceiving, and oppressing others)*. It is acceptable to Him to honor people that achieve and earn great incomes and assets who do so in accordance with His will. Yet, there are many believers pleasing Him who never amassed a million dollars. They should also be honored due to their labor of love for the LORD, fellow believers, and the lost. Never be a respecter-of-persons who ridicules or looks down on them. After all, many of them are probably helping your work and ministry endeavors succeed with their labors and giving.

Praise those who engage mission's ministry and those that faithfully serve and give in the local fellowship and community to evangelize and make disciples of other people at home and abroad. This includes the many people that to the natural eye don't seem to be doing anything great or worthy of accolades, yet they are faithful in helping ministries be great at doing what is necessary to affect and infect the world for Christ, leading them to salvation and eternal life.

While men can do things on earth that may be praised because it helps other people in some way *(provides jobs, find technologies that make work easier, help homeless people, etc.)*, we must understand that Christians are those whose communication and lifestyles lift up the LORD Jesus Christ and point to Him as Savior, from the wrath satan and those who remain unbelievers will bring upon themselves.

Abundant living that scripture speaks of is not based on reaching a million-dollar status, yet having more than enough money to do all that He called you to do will be an intricate part of it. He does not want you poor, broke, and in financial turmoil. Thus, the Holy Spirit speaks to us about good stewardship, in accordance with the bible, and desires that we pursue character development, spending habits, and lifestyles that employ it. You can be the blessed and highly favored one who can be a far greater blessing to many other people, just like He designed.

Please email me at rparlo@ameritech.net or call 517-393-5081 so I can forward a sample Net Worth Statement and Giving Saving Spending Plan *(budget)* you can use to eliminate financial bondage and powerfully build wealth.

Appendices 1 Thru 5 Are On The Follow Pages.

APPENDIX 1

INCOME & EXPENSE INFORMATION

Below is the type of information to gather for budget detail and financial planning.

All pay period gross income by source (employer, child support, other)

All pay period net income by source

Amounts per pay period put in savings and investments

All savings account values by source

All investment account values by source

All retirement account values by source

Description and value of all other assets that could be sold for cash *(real estate, rental homes, art, etc.)*

Annual federal, state, city income tax refund or payment

Total Tithe you paid last year

Total Offering you paid last year *(including faith promises, pledges, missions, everything to your Church, other Churches, and para-Church ministries)*

Total Other charitable contributions you paid last year to other organizations *(United Way, etc.)*

All debt totals, associated annual interest charges, monthly minimum payment, and monthly due dates for:

Home loans *(Mortgage, Home Equity Loan, etc. - separate for each property)*
Monthly Rent
Home insurance *(if not included in mortgage payment)*
Renters Insurance
Electric for home
Water for home
Gas for home
Home phone
Mobile phone
Car Loan
Car Insurance
Gas for car
Life Insurance
Disability Insurance
Personal Loans
Credit Cards *(Visa, Mastercard, Macy's, JCPenney, Younkers, etc.)*
Other debts owed to anyone or any entity
Groceries & household needs each pay period
Personal money for each family member each pay period
Miscellaneous spending each pay period
Amount put in emergency fund each pay period
Amount put in other savings and investment accounts each pay period

The items listed below encompass the types of things you may spend on during each month or calendar year. It will help you recall every type of expense particular to your situation, so you can put together accurate consecutive monthly budgets for the next year. You should have copies of the last two billing statements for each account available when you complete your consecutive monthly budgets, because this will give you a better idea of the estimated costs to include when any amounts due are not static for each account's monthly due date. When particular bills, are only due quarterly, semi-annually, or annually please include them using appropriate due dates in your budget.

APPENDIX 2

FINANCIAL INFO, NET WORTH STATEMENT, VISION & GOALS - EXAMPLE

Gross and net income amounts and before tax investment deductions

Business / Employer	Annual Gross Pay	Annual Net Pay	Monthly Gross Pay	Monthly Net Pay	401k, 403b, etc. Deduction
State of Michigan	$49,200	$36,000	$4,100	$ 3,000	$20
Michigan State Univ	$49,200	$36,000	$4,100	$3,000	$20
Ebay	$3,996	$2,400	$333	$200	_____
_____	_____	_____	_____	_____	_____

All Savings

Name of Institution	$Amount of Savings
AB&T	$ 350
_____	_____
_____	_____
_____	_____

All Retirement Accounts

Name of Institution	$Amount of Investment
State of Michigan 401k	$ 6,000
Michigan State 403b	$ 4,000

All Other Investments / Assets

Name of Institution / Item	$Amount of Investment / Asset
House	$400,000
Inherited land	$ 20,000
Chevy Camaro	$ 40,000
Ford Tempo	$ 25,000

Homes, cars, and other property can be an asset with a liability attached to them. The asset portion *(value of item)* should be listed above whereas the liability portion *(total debt owed on them)* should be listed below in the **All bills totals… section.**

Total of All Savings, Retirement Accounts, & Other Investments $495,350

All bill totals, expense categories, annual interest charge, and monthly payments

You should complete the chart below to show the total of all your spending, savings, and or investments that come out of your net income on a monthly basis. *(Tithe, Offering, Other charitable contributions, Other gifts, Groceries, Gas for heating, Electric, Water, Savings, Investment, Telephone, Internet connection, Home mortgage, Monthly Rent, Home / renters Insurance, Car Note, Car Insurance, Gas for car, Life Insurance, Disability Insurance, Personal Loans, Home loans, Credit Cards (Visa, MasterCard, Macy's, JCPenney, etc.), Clothing, Miscellaneous spending, and Other debts owed to anyone or any entity)*

Number of Months Until Paid Off is calculated by dividing your Total Owed by the Minimum Monthly Payment. For example, a Total Owed of $10,000 divided by a Minimum Monthly Payment of $200 will take at least 50 months *(over 4 years)* without counting interest added each month. It helps you see the need to correct your financial stewardship and situation.

Creditor to whom debt is owed	$ Total Owed	%Interest Rate	$ Minimum Monthly Payment	Monthly Due Date (1st, 3rd, etc)	Number of Months Until Paid Off
Mortgage	$ 340,000	5.1%	$ 1,100	3rd	309+
GMAC/camaro	$ 49,200	7.9%	$ 600	5th	82+
Ford/tempo	$ 34,800	7.5%	$ 410	7th	85+
Visa Card #1	$ 5,000	21.9%	$ 100	8th	50+
Visa Card #2	$ 5,500	17.9%	$ 110	10th	50+
MasterCard	$ 2,500	18.9%	$ 50	13th	50+
Discover	$ 5,000	22.9%	$ 100	16th	50+
Marshall Fields	$ 1,000	23.9%	$ 20	18th	50+
JCPenney	$ 1,000	24.9%	$ 20	21st	50+
Sak's Fifth Avenue	$ 3,500	25.9%	$ 70	23rd	50+
Mobile	$ 750	25.9%	$ 15	25th	50+
Shell	$ 750	24.9%	$ 15	26th	50+

Total of all **debt** listed above **$449,000**

Net Worth Statement

Assets	Liabilities	
(Total of **All Savings, Retirement Accounts, & Other Investments**)	(Total of all **debt** owed column above)	
$ 495,350	minus $ 449,000	equals $ 46,350, which is your financial **Net Worth**

Unfortunately, this may be a negative number for you right now but that can change with the Christ-like vision, a plan, and diligence to follow the plan!

Vision for your life and future

Write down the vision for your life *(what does the LORD want you to achieve during your lifetime)*. A Financial Freedom Plan sets goals and actions in place that help you obtain the amount of income, resources, and wealth accumulation that move you step by step to achieve the vision.

I plan to own 30 rental properties within the next ten years and give at least 20% of my gross income to the Church.

_____

_____

_____

Near term goals to pursue the vision (1-3 years)

   1. **Get finances in order by finding out my financial condition and budgeting to propel me.**

   2. _____

   3. _____

Mid-term goals to pursue the vision (4-7 years)

1. <u>**Start looking for properties I can buy for cash, fix up,**</u>
   <u>**and rent or sell for profit.**</u>

2. _____

3. _____

Long-term goals to pursue the vision (8 or more years)

1. <u>**Have at least $200,000 in no load, low expense total**</u>
   <u>**stock market index mutual funds.**</u>

2. _____

3. _____

APPENDIX 3

FINANCIAL INFO, NET WORTH STATEMENT, VISION & GOALS - BLANK WORKSHEET

All pay period gross and net income amounts and before tax savings deductions

Business/Employer	Annual Gross Pay	Annual Net Pay	Monthly Gross Pay	Monthly Net Pay	401k, 403b, etc. Deduction
_____	_____	_____	_____	_____	_____
_____	_____	_____	_____	_____	_____
_____	_____	_____	_____	_____	_____
_____	_____	_____	_____	_____	_____

All Savings

Name of Institution	$Amount of Savings
_____	_____
_____	_____
_____	_____
_____	_____

All Retirement Accounts

Name of Institution   *$Amount of Investment*

_____   _____

_____   _____

_____   _____

_____   _____

All Other Investments / Assets

Name of Institution/Item   *$Amount of Investment / Asset*

_____   _____

_____   _____

_____   _____

_____   _____

Homes, cars, and other property can be an asset with a liability attached to them. The asset portion *(value of item)* should be listed above whereas the liability portion *(total debt owed on them)* should be listed below in the **All bills totals… section.**

Total of **All Savings, Retirement
      Accounts, & Other Investments** $_____

All bill totals, expense categories, annual interest charge, and monthly payments

You should complete the chart below to show the total of all your spending, savings, and or investments that come out of your net income on a monthly basis. *(Tithe, Offering, Other charitable contributions, Other gifts, Groceries, Gas for heating, Electric, Water, Savings, Investment, Telephone, Internet connection, Home mortgage, Monthly Rent, Home / renters Insurance, Car Note, Car Insurance, Gas for car, Life Insurance, Disability Insurance, Personal Loans, Home loans, Credit Cards (Visa, MasterCard, Macy's, JCPenney, etc.), Clothing, Miscellaneous spending, and Other debts owed to anyone or any entity)*

Number of Months Until Paid Off is calculated by dividing your Total Owed by the Minimum Monthly Payment. For example, a Total Owed of $10,000 divided by a Minimum Monthly Payment of $200 will take at least 50 months *(over 4 years)* without counting interest added each month. It helps you see the need to correct your financial stewardship and situation.

Creditor to whom debt is owed	*$Total Owed*	*%Interest Rate*	*$Minimum Monthly Payment*	*Monthly Due Date (1ˢᵗ, 3ʳᵈ, etc)*	**Number of Months Until Paid Off**

Total of all **debt listed above** $_____

Net Worth Statement

Assets	Liabilities
(Total of **All Savings, Retirement Accounts, & Other Investments**)	(Total of all **debt** owed column above)

$ _____   **minus** $ _____   **equals** $ _____, which is your financial **Net Worth**

Unfortunately, this may be a negative number for you right now but that can change with the Christ-like vision, a plan, and diligence to follow the plan!

Vision for your life and future

Write down the vision for your life *(what does the LORD want you to achieve during your lifetime)*. A Financial Freedom Plan sets goals and actions in place that help you obtain the amount of income, resources, and wealth accumulation that move you step by step to achieve the vision.

_____

_____

_____

_____

_____

Near term goals to pursue the vision (1-3 years)

1. _____
2. _____
3. _____

Mid-term goals to pursue the vision (4-7 years)

1. _____
2. _____
3. _____

Long-term goals to pursue the vision (8 or more years)

1. _____
2. _____
3. _____

APPENDIX 4

EXAMPLE BUDGET

This is a sample budget that helps you identify how to fill in your budget.

EXAMPLE BUDGET FOR JOE & SARA SPENDER

Pay Period Surplus or Deficit (1)	$ 0
Pay Period Net Income (2)	$ 6,000
Other Income *(unexpected gifts, dividends, etc.)* (3)	$ 200
Total Disposable Income (4) = 1+2+3	$ 6,200

<u>Tithe</u> *(10% of your gross income)*	$ 820
<u>Offering</u> *(amount you desire from your heart)*	$ 410
Savings	$ 500
Mortgage	$ 1,100
Property Tax	_____
Home Insurance	_____
Home Maintenance	_____
Car Loan #1	$ 600
Car Loan #2	$ 410
Car Maintenance	_____
Visa Card #1	$ 100
Visa Card #2	$ 110
MasterCard	$ 50
Discover	$ 100
Marshall Fields	$ 20

JC Penney	$ 20
Sac's Fifth Avenue	$ 70
Mobile	$ 15
Shell	$ 15
Gas for home	$ 50
Electric	$ 20
Water/Sewage	$ 10
Telephone	$ 100
Cable Television	$ 50
Internet Connection *(DSL)*	$ 50
Daycare	$ 500
After School Programs	$ 200
Groceries	$ 300
Husband's Personal Money	$ 500
Wife's Personal Money	$ 500
Children's Allowance	$ 20
Clothing	_____
Medical care *(health, dental, etc.)*	_____
Entertainment *(movies, videos, plays, etc.)*	_____
_____	_____
_____	_____
_____	_____
Total Monthly Expenses (5)	$ 6640

Total Disposable Income (4) - Total Monthly Expenses (5) = $ (440)

Surplus or Deficit

172

APPENDIX 5

BLANK BUDGET WORKSHEET

This is a blank budget form for creating your monthly budget. Copy enough to complete at least three months of budgets or replicate it on an excel spreadsheet.

Pay Period Surplus or Deficit (1)   _____

Pay Period Net Income (2)   _____

Other Income *(unexpected gifts, dividends, etc.)* (3)   _____

Total Disposable Income (4) = 1+2+3   _____

<ins>Tithe</ins> *(10% of your gross income)*   _____

<ins>Offering</ins> *(amount desired to give from your heart)*   _____

_____   _____

_____   _____

_____   _____

_____   _____

_____   _____

_____   _____

_____   _____

_____   _____

_____   _____

_____   _____

_____   _____

_____ _____

_____ _____

_____ _____

_____ _____

_____ _____

_____ _____

_____ _____

_____ _____

_____ _____

_____ _____

_____ _____

_____ _____

_____ _____

_____ _____

_____ _____

_____ _____

_____ _____

_____ _____

_____ _____

_____ _____

Total Monthly Expenses (5)   _____

Total Disposable Income (4) - Total Monthly Expenses (5) =   _____

                                                            Surplus or Deficit

Printed in the United States
By Bookmasters